great songs... of the seventies volume 1

edited by **milton okun**

ISBN 0-8129b-311-3

Visit our website at www.cherrylane.com

Acknowledgments

I would like to express my thanks to my friends and associates for their invaluable assistance and suggestions: Jean Dinegar, Dan Fox, and Murray Frank; and special thanks to Dan Rosenbaum, John Stix, and Mark Phillips, without whose encouragement and prodding I might still be mulling over titles and decisions instead of deadlines!

Also, my appreciation to Hal Leonard and those publishers and writers who have cooperated so generously in making this collection possible.

I would like to express my gratitude to those publishers who were willing to cooperate but were unable to do so because of contractual obligations.

Introduction

A song, by definition, is a short poem intended for singing. This seems clear enough. But a song is distinguished from other poems by its free use of rhythm and rhyme, by its directness and by its simplicity of sentiment. And a song is always lyrical.

Western wind,
when will thou blow?
The small rain down can rain.
Christ, that my love were
in my arms,
And I in my bed again,

Anonymous,
Perhaps the earliest
song in English

I should immediately distinguish between lyrical and happy. Songs are not always happy songs; sadness and lamentation have a lyricism of their own that has been captured in song — classical, folk and popular. Classical songs and songs of the opera that project direct (sometimes profound) human emotions in a lyrical manner we call *grand.* But we call *great* those songs that are accessible to the nonprofessional and to the untrained music lover. The great songs, the enduring songs, are those that are playable by a pianist, a guitarist, an organist, or nearly anyone. The great songs are those that can be sung by the untrained voice, by one who has no idea what his octave range is. The great songs last because people do use them.

And this brings me to the paradox of the songs of the seventies. The seventies represent, at least to this moment, the greatest development in the *sound* of recording. The technological and electronic advancement in the recording industry is almost beyond belief. If there is a technique now lacking that will make a shallow song seem on first hearing to be powerful, exciting and strong, then the technicians will invent that technique tomorrow. We all suffer a barrage of technically superior noise created by virtuostic musicians supported by electronic technicians.

This electronic hyping of bad songs made the selection of the *Great Songs of the Seventies* sometimes a tedious task. It wasn't so much a search for a needle in a haystack as it was a search for the golden nugget in the swirling sands of the prospector's tin pan. But golden nuggets I found in the songs of the seventies.

I see the whole seventies as a time of paradox, and the first paradox is this: As the recording industry moved forward toward electronic sophistication, the songwriters moved back toward more simple statements about human relations. Soon enough historians of contemporary music, and particularly of that wondrous phenomenon, the Beatles, will point out that there is a direct, traceable movement from the Beatles' earliest recordings to the present offering of Paul McCartney's Wings; but the real truth is that McCartney's seventies offering, "My Love," is, in its structure and simplicity of statement, closer to the fourteenth century song "Western Wind, When Will Thou Blow?" than it is to the earlier Beatles' song "Lucy In The Sky with Diamonds." All things move forward and backwards.

Here is another paradox: The songs of the seventies, while embracing the American Dream ("Thank God I'm a Country Boy") have moved away from what was once thought of as a sacred American tradition: Tin Pan Alley.

Once upon a time Tin Pan Alley gave us our songs, and those songs delineated and limited the boundaries of our emotions. They were good songs: "I Get a Kick Out of You," "Let's Fall in Love," "I Can't Get Started with You." Generations of Americans danced to the tunes of Tin Pan Alley and hummed the melodies of the professional songwriters. In 1978, the 90-year-old Irving Berlin celebrated his more than seventy years of songwriting. But the sixties challenged the importance of the professional songwriter and by now, in the seventies, we can say that their era is over. The songwriters represented here in *Great Songs of the Seventies* come not just from Hollywood and New York but from almost every section of the English speaking world, and from many segments of society. Looking back, I suppose we can see that the Beatles' Liverpuddlian song, "Rita the Meter Maid," was really a challenge to the sophisticated lyrics of Cole Porter and Noel Coward. The sixties saw the Beatles as the Challengers, and what the sixties witnessed, the seventies prove: The

Beatles did not replace one dominant style of songwriting with another. They led us all on to *diversity*. They opened the way for the songwriters who were just youngsters who loved to sing, who loved to write; youngsters who knew nothing about the right way to approach a song publisher but knew their way around a recording studio. They wrote their own songs, experimented with four-track and eight-track, with synthesizers and echo chambers; they gathered their groups, cut records and appealed directly to the public rather than to music publishers or music producers who too often regarded them with contempt. It was a revolution in the sixties and it is a commonplace observation in the seventies: Songwriters come from all sectors of the country and from all musical impulses — rock, folk, soul, disco, and theater. And yet, even as I write this I can see that those distinctions are beginning to blur: Disco is heavily indebted to rock, and some of the finest guitar-based rock music is indebted to Kern, Porter, Berlin, and Gershwin. Reflecting on this era of change, it seems not unlike the conflict in Wagner's *Die Meistersinger* where the old guard, the guild of mastersingers, is challenged by a new young talent who successfully takes his place in the musical process but only by incorporating the wisdom and traditions of his elders.

The dominant force in the sixties was, of course, the Beatles. At that time there was nearly endless speculation as to where the wonderful creative drive came from: Was it McCartney or Lennon? Could Ringo Starr be the catalyst or was it the quiet one, George Harrison? After the breakup of the Beatles, Paul McCartney and John Lennon continued careers of superior songwriting. Although some of John Lennon's songs might be called masterpieces, he has not achieved the international success of Paul McCartney. I admit to personal bias in the selection of the *Great Songs of the Seventies*, but I think that it can be justly said: Of the four Beatles, McCartney and Lennon have sustained their brilliance into the seventies.

Before moving on I want to say something about Elvis. Though not represented in the *Great Songs of the Seventies*, his professional life can be seen as almost a model of the course of popular music in America since the late fifties. He was the leader in the movement towards democratization of popular music. His first recording, a simple tribute to his mother, was made in a rented recording booth. The small company that picked up his first record made its appeal not to the moguls and entrepreneurs of the music establishment but directly to the public who embraced Elvis.

Elvis was the one who taught a generation of kids how to move the body to the beat of frenzied, urgent music. All of the performers of soul music owe a debt to Elvis. Since his death his fans have tried to make a monument of him. Bumper stickers read "The King Is Dead," but Elvis is a living legacy in the seventies. For the whole of the disco craze is his legacy. The frenetic movements to song, the exhibitionist dance have, in the seventies, simply moved from the stage to the dance floor. *Saturday Night Fever* is the "Son of Elvis."

What surprised me in my review of the songs of the seventies was how solid, how really good are so many of these songs. I didn't expect such value, given the electronic hyping, the cross-fertilization of soul and rock with the old 32-bar song, and the emphasis on dance-oriented disco music — given all these facts, who would expect "good" songs? And yet they are. Many disco songs that I expected to find repetitive and uninteresting were rhythmic and strong. When played simply on the piano, these songs have strong melodies. Some have moving or interesting lyrics with melodies that have a special catch. There are interesting harmonic progressions and often surprising structures. Many of the songs have a simple charm that was not to be discovered in their complex, sound-dominated recordings.

Over and over again I have been amazed at the vision and passion in the works of the new songwriters, many not musically trained, whose dreams come forth in song with moving intensity. In this collection of songs there are moments that seem commonplace and ordinary, but there are also moments of extraordinary wisdom and beauty and insight. I am not quite ready to say that this is a Golden Age of Songwriting but here is a body of work to be respected.

Although the songs of the seventies obviously derive from the songs of the sixties (the same impulses are at work), I do find one significant difference. The songs of the seventies are not didactic, nor are they tied to social causes. Here there is nothing quite like the social protest of Pete Seeger's "Where Have All the Flowers Gone?" Or "Little Boxes" ("ticky-tacky, and they all just look the same"). An astonishing number of the songs are songs of simple, romantic love ("My Love," "The First Time Ever I Saw Your Face"). The songs of social protest take such a curious turn that I shall reserve discussion of this to a later point.

I come to still another paradox: Although the traditional bases of the songs tend to fuse (rock into disco and jazz into soul), the public presentation of the songs divides into two quite different modes: sophisticated or folk.

At a large charity banquet, at which two great performers appeared, the two modes of presentation were demonstrated. First Diana Ross sang a set with a large orchestra accompanying her. Her costumes (she made one change between songs), the lighting, the dramatic effect of the full brass and rhythm sections were intoxicating and she came off the stage to a thunderous ovation. She was followed by John Denver who sang three songs accompanied by only his own six-string guitar. His songs were simple and he closed with "America the Beautiful." The simplicity, the musical, rhythmic, and harmonic rightness were even more overpowering and intense than the much larger, complex sound of Diana Ross. Every word that Denver sang, every quiet chord or note of the guitar resounded in the listener's head. It was a profound lesson to me in the power of "song."

I think that it might be fun to vary your approach to the song styles in this collection. Some of the rock songs stand up remarkably well when treated as ballads. Let me suggest Rod Stewart's "Maggie May" or the Bee Gees "Love So Right" and "Nights on Broadway." It would be equally interesting to take some of the slow ballads and treat them in a modified rock fashion. Billy Joel's "Just the Way You Are" would be a good place to start.

All of the songs in this collection were successful. Many of them were gigantic successes, listened to by millions of people. At one time in my life I was suspicious of that kind of popularity. I thought that great composers were discovered only after their deaths. But as I grow older I learn. Mozart, Schubert, Brahms, Beethoven, Bach — these were not undiscovered geniuses. They knew the audience they were writing for and they wanted their music to be accessible. Great music is usually popular music. In his eightieth year, Giuseppe Verdi gave this wise advice to a young composer: "Look to the box office."

Two of the giants of the sixties who have continued their development, and are represented in this collection by more than one song, are Bob Dylan and John Denver. Other writers of the seventies who began their work in the sixties, or found their inspiration in the music of that period are Billy Joel, Elton John, and Bernie Taupin. As the music of the sixties was dominated by rock, the music of the seventies responds to the powerful influence of disco. The way disco absorbs earlier influences can be heard in the music of the Australian Brothers Gibb's *Saturday Night Fever*, whose early songs were folk oriented, then became rock oriented, and are now disco.

But there is a significant difference between this collection and *Great Songs of the Sixties*. That collection was advertised as "a social document you can play on your piano." And it is true that the sixties were the years when the great social movements found voice in song. The youth movement, the civil rights struggle, and the anti-war demonstrations were supported by the music community. Many songwriters of that era made their biggest impact with protest songs. No one was really surprised to find Peter, Paul and Mary with the demonstrators at the Chicago Democratic Convention. And no one who heard Pete Seeger sing "We Shall Overcome" is apt to forget the haunting, compelling power of that quiet song.

This collection of 70 songs of the seventies makes few direct references to social issues. Jim Croce's "Bad, Bad Leroy Brown" is not a cry against inner-city blight. The dominant feature of the songs of this decade is the personal, internal search for self or the meaning of life. Janis Ian's "At Seventeen" and Norman Gimbel and Charles Fox's "Killing Me Softly with His Song" are both powerful explorations of personal yearning.

And this is the last paradox of the songs of the seventies. At a time when political corruption threatened to overturn an entire government, when Watergate was on every tongue, when the President of the United States was found to have an Enemies List, the songwriters turned away from protest to an affirmation of the goodness of life, the joy of responsible love, the happiness that the individual can find in naturalness. John Denver's "Rocky Mountain High" and his "Sunshine on My Shoulders" are not protests against corruption. They are a reply to it, a reaffirmation of the supremacy of goodness and the importance of love. It is the love and yearning of "Western Wind, When Will Thou Blow?"

These are good songs, the songs of the seventies. I hope that they will bring enjoyment for many years to come to the people who play them and sing them.

— Milton Okun

Milton Okun

Milton Okun, legendary record producer, arranger, and founder of Cherry Lane Music Company, was born in New York City. He received his BS in Music Education from New York University, his Masters of Education from the Oberlin Conservatory of Music, and taught music in the New York City public school system early in his career.

Among his numerous and varied associations, Okun was the arranger and conductor for Harry Belafonte, and the arranger and producer for Peter, Paul and Mary, as well as the Chad Mitchell Trio, before embarking on his historic association with John Denver as producer, musical director and publisher. Among Okun's prized recordings are those with Placido Domingo. Okun was also the arranger of the classic collection, The Compleat Beatles, *and has earned 46 gold and platinum records.*

CONTENTS

After The Love Has Gone

Words and Music by David Foster, Jay Graydon and Bill Champlin

Fsus2/A
Dm7
young and we knew, and our eyes were a - live
ev - er need. Love was strong for so long,
B♭maj7
E♭6/9
deep in - side we knew our love
nev - er knew that what was wrong,
C7sus
C7
F
B♭m/F
was true. For a while we paid no mind to the past,
ba - by, was - n't right. We tried to find what we had
F
Gm7
G♯m7
Fsus2/A
Dm7
we knew love would last. Ev - 'ry night some - thin'
'til sad - ness was all we shared. We were

B♭maj7
C9sus
C7
right would in - vite us to be - gin the dance.
scared this af - fair would lead our love in - to.
B♭maj7
F/A
Dm7
Gm7
3fr
To Coda I
Some - thin' hap-pened a - long the way; what used to be hap - py was sad.
Some - thin' hap-pened a - long the way; yes - ter - day was all we had.
F
Amaj7/B
Emaj7
B/D♯
4fr
G♯m7
4fr
Some - thin' hap-pened a - long the way and
C♯m7
4fr
Bmaj9
yes - ter - day was all we had. And

Cm7
3fr
Fm7
Bbm7
oh,
af - ter the love has gone,
Eb9sus
6fr
Eb9
Abm7
4fr
Db9sus
Db9
how could you lead me on
and not let me stay a - round?
Gbmaj9
3fr
Abm7
4fr
Bbm7
Cm7
3fr
Oh,
Fm7
Bbm7
Eb9sus
6fr
Eb9
af - ter the love has gone
what used to be right was wrong.

A♭m7
4fr
D♭9sus
D♭9
To Coda II
Can love that's lost be found?
G♭maj7
E/F♯
C9sus
C7♭9
D.S. al Coda I
For a - while
CODA I
F
B9♯11
B♭maj7
Some - thin' hap - pened a - long
F/A
Dm7
Gm7
3fr
D.S.S. al Coda
F
Amaj7/B
the way; what used to be hap - py is sad.

CODA II
G♭maj7
A♭m7
B♭m7
C♭maj9
D♭m7
Oh,
E♭m7
Fm7
B♭m7
Oh, af - ter the love has gone,
E♭m7
A♭9sus
A♭9
C♯m7
what used to be right was wrong. Can
Repeat and Fade
F♯9sus
Bmaj7
C♯m7
E♭m7
love that's lost be found? Oh.

Afternoon Delight

Words and Music by Bill Danoff

D7
C7
thing's a lit - tle clear - er in the light of day,
Am7
Gm7
D7
C7
And we know the night is al - ways gon - na be here an - y - way?
G
F
1.3. Think - ing of you's work - ing up my ap - pe - tite, look - ing
2. out this morn - ing feel - ing so po - lite, I al - ways
Am7
Gm7
for - ward to a lit - tle af - ter - noon de - light. Rub - bing
thought a fish could not be caught who did - n't bite. But you

G
F
sticks and stones to - geth - er make the sparks ig - nite And the
got some bait a - wait - ing and I think I might Like
Am7
Gm7
G
F
thought of rub - bing you is get - ting so ex - cit - ing.
nib - bl - ing a lit - tle af - ter - noon de - light.
Sky rock - ets in
D
B7
Em
C
A7
Dm
flight, Af - ter - noon de - light,
Am7
Bm
C
D7
G
Gm7
Am
B♭
C7
F
af - ter - noon de - light,

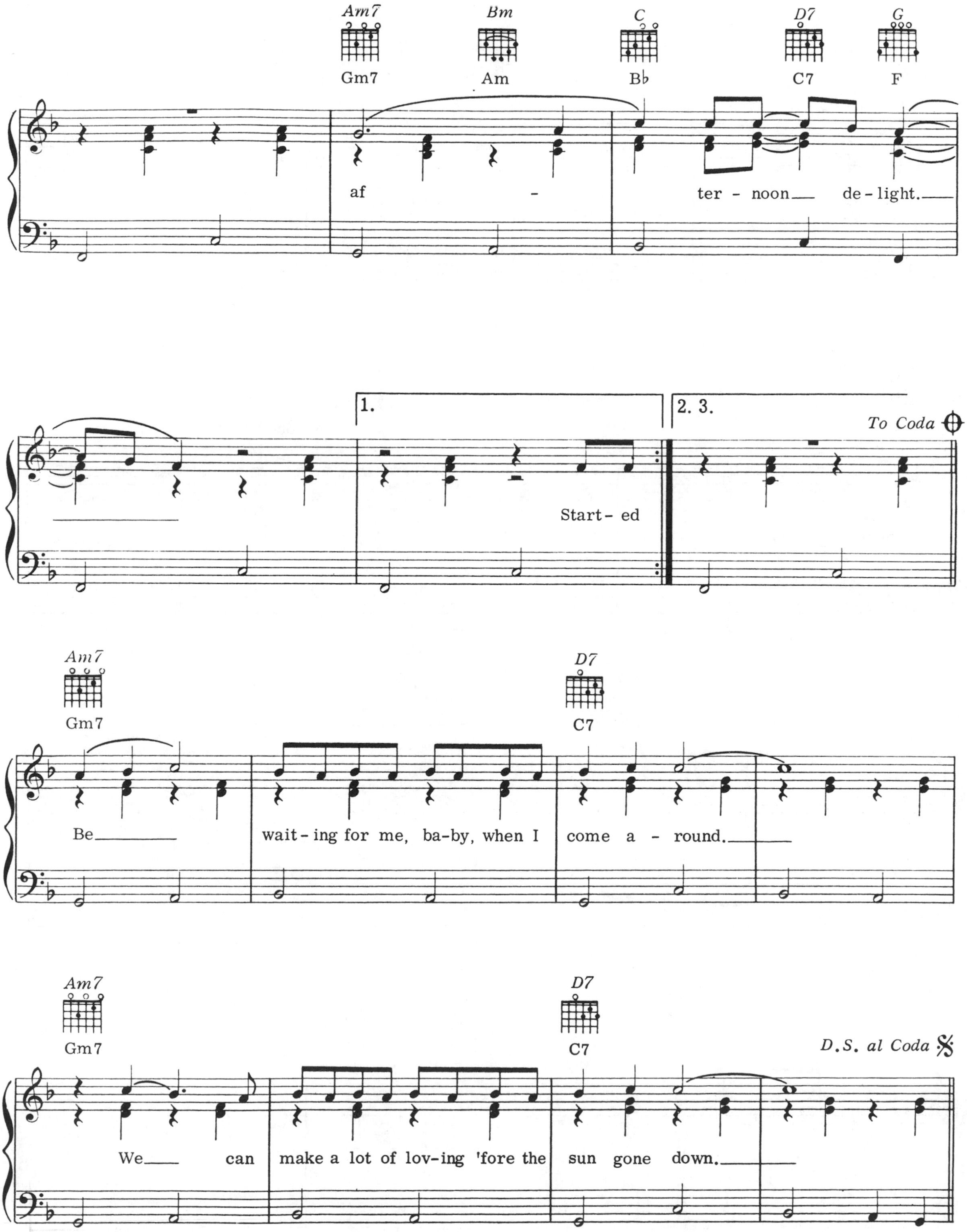

Am7 Bm C D7 G

Gm7 Am B♭ C7 F

af - ter - noon de - light.

1. 2. 3. *To Coda*

Start - ed

Am7 D7

Gm7 C7

Be wait - ing for me, ba - by, when I come a - round.

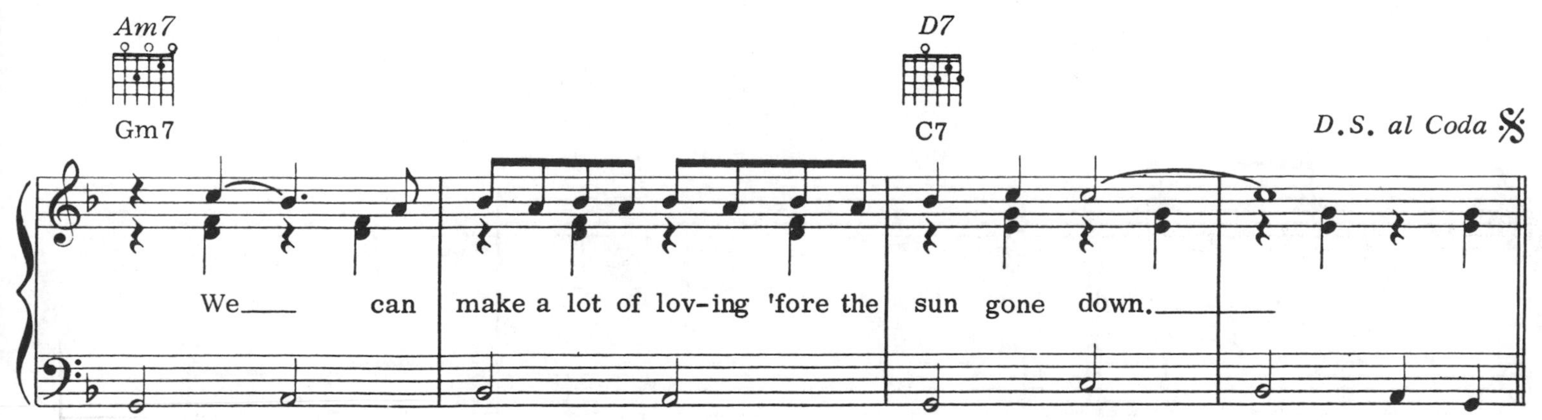
Am7
D7
Gm7
C7
D.S. al Coda
We can make a lot of lov - ing 'fore the sun gone down.

Coda
Am
Bm
C
D
Gm
Am
B♭
C
af - - - af - ter - noon de - light,
G
F
No chords
af - -
- - - -
G
F
af - ter - noon de - light.

At Seventeen

Words and Music by Janis Ian

C
Dm
val - en-tines I nev - er knew, the Fri - day night cha - rades
rich re - la - tioned home - town queen mar - ries in - to what
long a - go and far a - way. The world was young - er than
G7
of youth were spent on one more beau - ti - ful At
she needs A guar - an - tee of com - pa - ny And
to - day and dreams were all they gave for free to
C
sev - en-teen, I learned the truth. And
ha - ven for the eld - er - ly." Re -
ug - ly duck-ling girls like me. We all
Eb
3 fr.
Dm7
those of us with rav - aged fac - es, lack-ing in the so -
mem - ber those who win the game lose the love they sought
play the game and when we dare to cheat our-selves at sol -

G7
Cm7
3 fr.
Fm7
- cial grac - es, Des - p'rate - ly re - mained at home in -
to gain In de - ben - tures of qual - i - ty and
- i - taire In - vent - ing lov - ers on the phone, re -
Cm7
3 fr.
Fm7
A♭
4 fr.
vent - ing lov - ers on the phone Who called to say, "Come dance
du - bi - ous in - teg - ri - ty. Their small town eyes will gape
pent - ing oth - er lives un - known, that call and say, "Come dance
G7
Cm7
3 fr.
Fm7
with me," and mur - mured vague ob - scen - i - ties.
at you in dull sur - prise when pay - ment due
with me," and mur - mur vague ob - scen - i - ties
Dm7
G7
1. 2.
It is - n't all it seems at sev - en - teen.
ex - ceeds ac - counts re - ceived at sev - en - teen.
at ug - ly girls like me at sev - en - teen.
2. A
3. To
3.
C
Cmaj7

Annie's Song

Words and Music by John Denver

A7
G
rain, Like a storm in the des -
A
Bm
G
D
D/C♯
ert, like a sleep - y blue o - cean,
D/B
D/A
G
F♯m
Em
You fill up my sen - ses, come
A7
D
Dsus4
D
Dsus4
fill me a - gain. Come let me

G
A
Bm
G
love you, let me give my life
sen - ses like a night in a
D
D/C♯
D/B
D/A
G
to you, Let me drown in your laugh -
for - est, Like the moun-tains in spring -
F♯m
Em
G
A7
ter, let me die in your arms.
time, like a walk in the rain.
G
A
Bm
Let me lay down be - side you, let me
Like a storm in the des - ert, like a
2nd time hold back---

G
D
D/C#
D/B
al - ways be with you,
sleep - y blue o - cean,
You
in tempo
D/A
G
F#m
Em
A7
Come let me love you,
come love me a -
fill up my sen - ses,
come fill me a -
1.
D
Dsus4
D
Dsus4
gain.
You fill up my
2.
D
gain.
dim.
Dsus4
D
Dsus4
D
Dsus4
D

Bad, Bad Leroy Brown

Words and Music by Jim Croce

A7
B7
stand 'bout six-foot - four;
All the down - town la - dies call him
El - do - ra - do, too;
He got a thir-ty-two gun in his
trou - ble soon be - gan,
And Le - roy Brown, he learned a
C
D7
G
"tree - top lov - er," all the men just call him, "Sir."
pock - et for fun, he got a ra - zor in his shoe.
les - son 'bout mess - in' with the wife of a jeal-ous man.
And he's bad,
Chorus
G
A7
bad Le-roy Brown, the bad-dest man in the whole damned town;
B7
C
D
C
To Coda
1. 2.
G
N. C.
bad-der than old King Kong and mean-er than a junk-yard dog.
2. Now Le-
3. Well, Fri-

3.
G
N. C.
G
A7
Well, the two men took to fight - in', and when they pulled them from the floor
B7
C
D7
Le-roy looked like a jig - saw puz - zle with a cou- ple of piec-es gone.
G
D. S. al Coda
And he's bad,
Coda
G
N. C.
B7
Yes, you were bad-der than old King Kong,
C
D
C
G
and mean-er than a junk-yard dog.

Band On The Run

Words and Music by McCartney

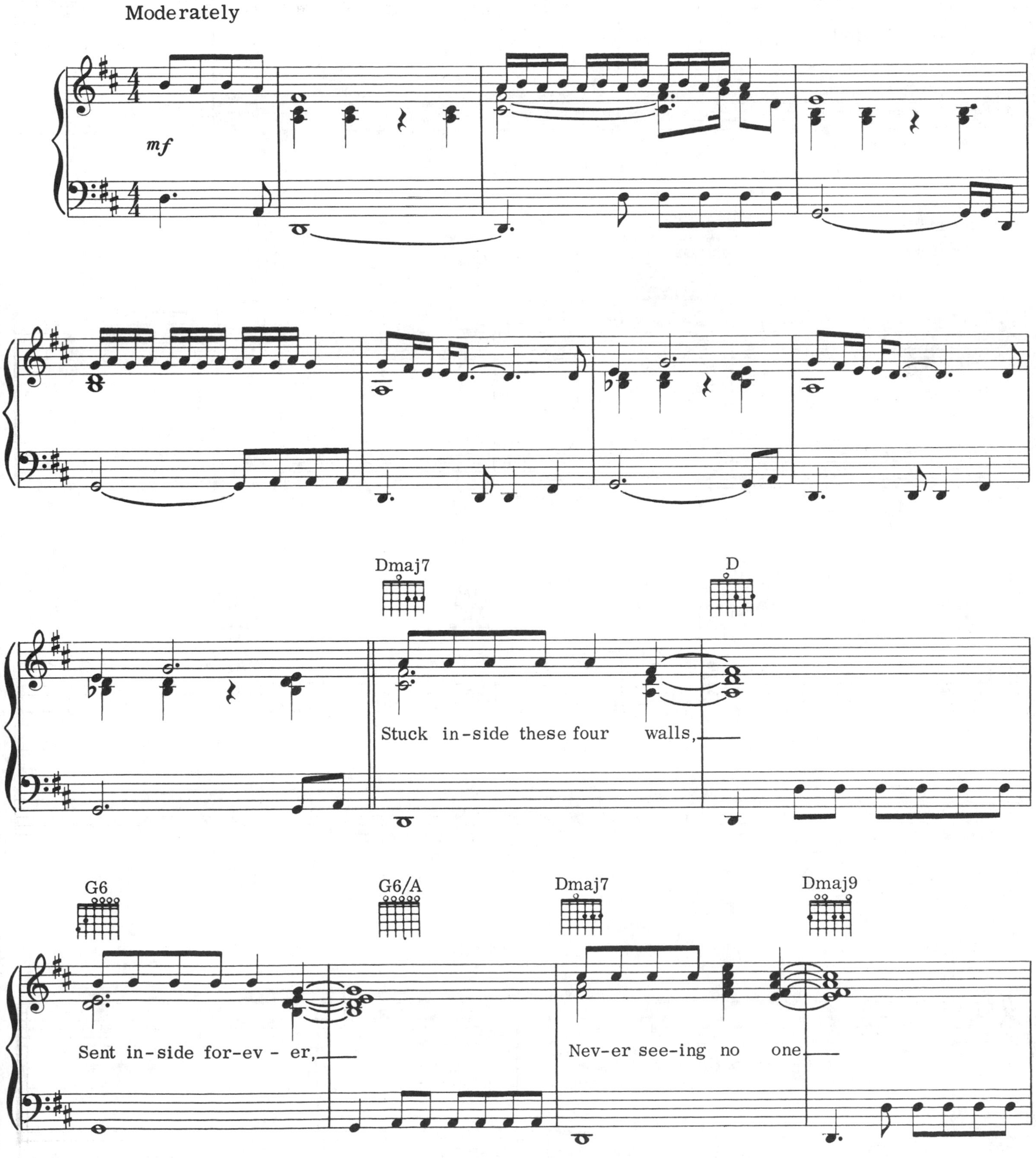

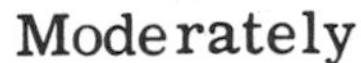

Moderately
mf
Dmaj7
D
Stuck in-side these four walls,
G6
G6/A
Dmaj7
Dmaj9
Sent in-side for-ev - er,
Nev-er see-ing no one

G
A
G
D
Gm6
G
D
nice a-gain
Like you,
ma-ma,
You,
Gm6
Dmaj7
Gm6
Am
ma-ma,
you.
D6
Am
D6
Am
Am
D
If I ev-er get out of here
Thought of giv-ing it all a-way

Am
D
To a reg-is-tered char - i - ty.
All I need is a pint_ a day If I
Am
ev-er get out_ of here,_ (If we ev-er get out_ of here.)_
Brighter beat
C
D5
C5
D5
C5
C
Fmaj7
C
Fmaj7
1. Well, the

C
Fmaj7
rain ex - plod - ed with a mighty - y crash As we fell in - to the sun,
un - der - tak - er drew a heav - y sigh See - ing no one else had come,
night was fall - ing as the des - ert world Be - gan to set - tle down.
C
Fmaj7
And the first one said to the sec - ond one there I
And a bell was ring - ing in the vil - lage square For the
In the town they're search - ing for us ev - 'ry where, But we
Em
G
C
hope you're hav - ing fun.
rab - bits on the run.
nev - er will be found.
Band on the run;
Em
C
Am
F
Band on the run;
1. 2. And the jail - er man and
3. And the coun - ty judge who

C
F
Fmaj7
N.C.
sail - or Sam Were search - ing ev - 'ry one
held a grudge Will search for ev - er more
For the
C
Band on the run,
Band on the run,
1. 2.
Band on the run,
Band on the run.
2. Well, the
3. Well, the
3.
Em
G
C
Band on the run.

Brand New Key

Words and Music by Melanie Safka

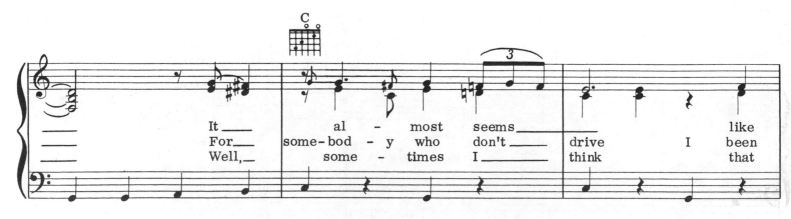

Moderately
mf lightly
C
I rode my bi-cy-cle past your win-dow last night,
I ride my bike, I roll-er-skate, don't drive no car,
I asked your moth-er if you were at home,
G7
I roll-er-skat-ed to your door at day-light,
Don't go too fast but I go pret-ty far,
She said yes, but you were-n't a-lone.
C
It al-most seems like
For some-bod-y who don't drive I been
Well, some-times I think that

F
G7
C
you're a - void - ing me,
all a - round the world,
you're a - void - ing me,
I'm o - kay a - lone,
Some peo - ple say
I'm o - kay a - lone
but you got some - thing I need: Well,
I done all right for a girl. Oh,
but you got some - thing I need: Well,
I
got a brand new pair of roll - er skates, you got a brand new
key,
I think that we should get to - geth - er and

F
try them out, you see.
I been look - ing a - round
a while,
you got some - thing for
me. Oh, I
G7
C
got a brand new
pair of roll - er skates,
you got a brand new
1. 2.
key.
3.
key.

Don't Let Me Be Lonely Tonight

Words and Music by James Taylor

B7sus4/F♯ B7 Gmaj7 D/F♯ Bm7 E7(9)
time to go. Don't say yes, but please don't say no, I don't
Em7(9) A7(6)sus4 Dmaj7(9) Dmaj7 Bm Bm(maj7)
want to be lone-ly to-night. Go a- way then, damn ya, go
Bm7 E7(9) Em7(9) A7(6)sus4 A7 C
on and do as you please, yeah, You ain't gon-na see me get-tin'
G D Bm Bm(maj7) Bm7 E7(9)
down on my knees. I'm un-de-cid-ed and your heart's been di-vid-ed, you've been
Em7(9) A7(6)sus4 A7 C G
N. C.
turn-in' my world up-side down.

Em7(9)
A7(6)sus4
Dmaj7(9)
B7-9/F♯
Em7(9)
A7(6)sus4
Do me wrong,
do me right, right now, ba - by.
Go on and tell me lies but
B7sus4/F♯
B7
Gmaj7
D/F♯
Bm7
E7(9)
hold me tight.
Save your good-byes for the morn - in' light,
But don't
Em7(9)
A7(6)sus4
C9+11
G
D/F♯
let me be lone - ly to - night.
I don't
want to be lone - ly to - night
Bm7
E7(9)
Em7(9)
A7(6)sus4
Dmaj7(9)
no, no, I don't
want to be lone - ly to - night.

Calypso

Words and Music by John Denver

A6
Amaj7
A
life and the liv - ing, In search of the an - swers to ques - tions un -
your si - lent world, To live on the land we must learn from the
Bm/A
A
known To be part of the move-ment and
sea, To be true as the tide And
A6
Amaj7
A
part of the grow - ing Part of be - gin - ning to un - der -
free as a wind - swell, Joy - ful and lov - ing in let - ting it
Em7/A
D
stand.
be.
ff
Aye, Ca-lyp - so, The

A D A E A
plac-es you've been to, The things that you've shown us, The sto-ries you tell!
Chorus
D A D A
Aye, Ca-lyp-so, I sing to your spi-rit, The men who have served you so
E7 A E D A
long and so well. Hi-dee-ay-ee-ooo do-dle-
E D A E
oh-ooo do do do do do do-dle-ay-ee

D
A
E
Dsus4
do-dle - ay - ee.
D
A
(add B)
A
f
D/A
A
(add B)
2nd time fade here
D/A
D.S. and fade
on Chorus
Like the

(They Long To Be)

Close To You

Lyric by Hal David
Music by Burt Bacharach

Abmaj7
G7sus
G7
Gm7
stars fall down from the sky ev-'ry time you walk
mp
Cm7
Ab
4fr
by? Just like me___ they long to be
mf
Eb6
Ebmaj7
Eb6
Ebmaj7
Ab
4fr
Ab6
Abmaj7
Ab6
close to you.___ On the day that you were born the
f

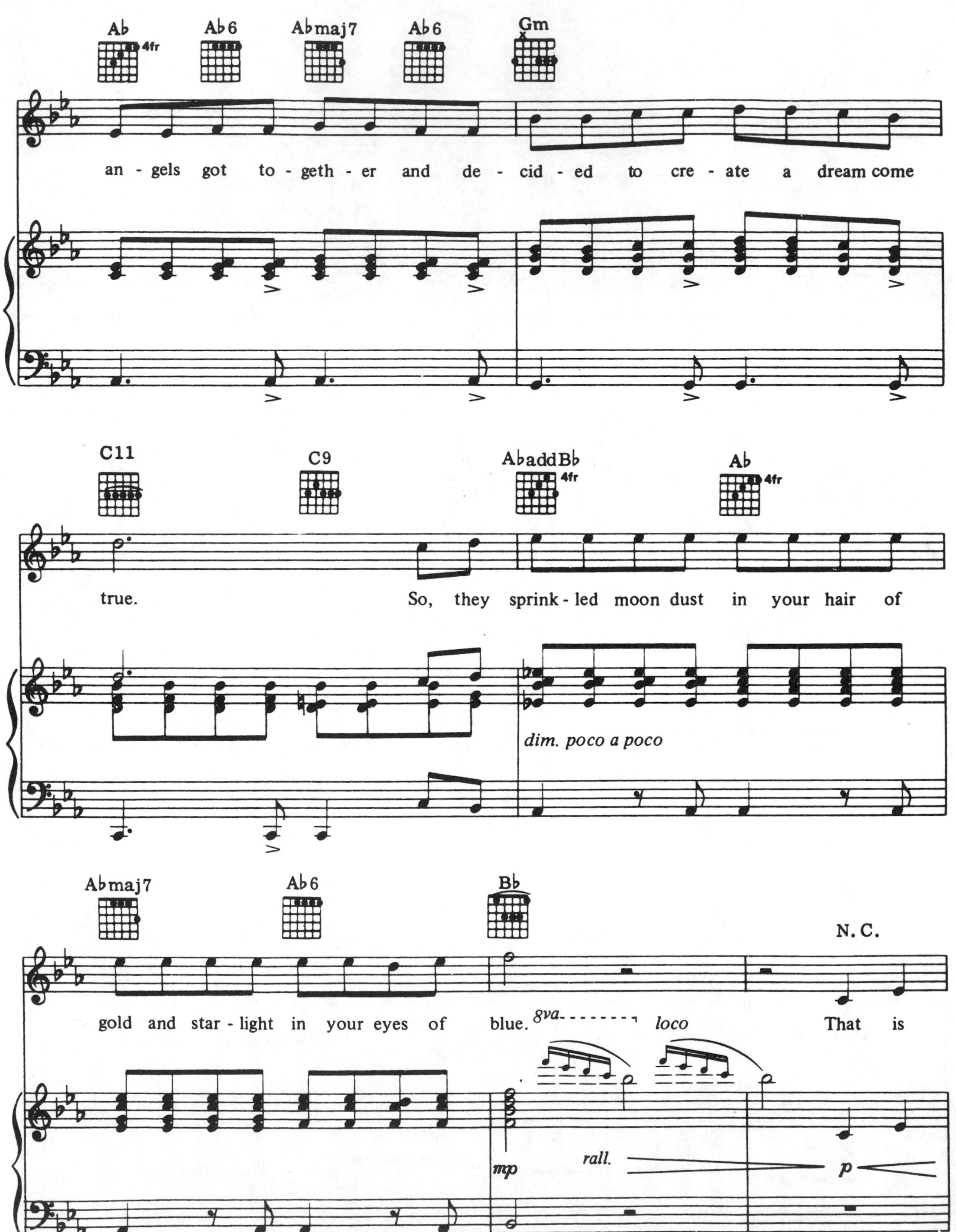
Ab
4fr
Ab6
Abmaj7
Ab6
Gm
an - gels got to - geth - er and de - cid - ed to cre - ate a dream come
C11
C9
AbaddBb
4fr
Ab
4fr
true. So, they sprink - led moon dust in your hair of
dim. poco a poco
Abmaj7
Ab6
Bb
N. C.
gold and star - light in your eyes of blue.
8va
loco
That is
mp
rall.
p

Abmaj7
G7sus
G7
Gm7
why all the {boys / girls} in town fol-low you all a-
mp a tempo
Cm7
Ab
4fr
round. Just like me_ they long to be
Eb6
Ebmaj7
Eb6
Ebmaj7
Ab
4fr
AbaddBb
4fr
close to you._ Just like me_
dim. poco a poco
Ab
4fr
AbaddBb
4fr
Eb6
Ebmaj7
Eb6
Ebmaj7
they long to be close to you._
keep repeating & fade out

Cold As Ice

Words and Music by Mick Jones and Lou Gramm

C6
C
C6
C
Am
Some-day you'll pay the price, I know. I've
G
F♯+
Am
seen it be-fore; it hap-pens all the time. You're clos-ing the door; you leave the
C
C/D
G
F♯+
world be-hind. You're dig-ging for gold yet throw-ing a-way a
Am
1.
B7
Emsus 4
Em
for-tune in feel-ings, but some-day you'll pay.
3
3

Emsus 4
Em
C6
C
C6
C
2.
B7
some-day you'll pay.
C
Em/B
C
Am
G
B
D
Em
B7/F♯
Cold
as

B7/A
No chord
ice. You know that you are.
Em
Cold (cold)
B7/F♯
as (as)
B7/A
N.C.
ice.
C
Emsus 4
Em
Emsus 4
Em
C6
C
C6
C
Ooh,
cold as, cold as
Repeat (with vocal ad lib) and fade
Emsus 4
Em
Emsus 4
Em
C6
C
C6
C
ice.
Cold as, cold as
Repeat and fade

Don't Let The Sun Go Down On Me

Words and Music by Elton John and Bernie Taupin

G7
F/C
C
F
and time stands still be- fore___ me,
Fro-zen here
G
C/G
G
C/G
on the lad - der of my life.
G7
C/G
G
C
Too late___
I can't find,
to save my- self from fall - ing,
oh, the right ro - man - tic line,
F
I took a chance
But see me once
and changed your way of
and see the way I

G7 C/G G G7
life. But you mis-read my mean-ing when I
feel. Don't dis-card me just be-cause you
F/C C F
met you, Closed the door
think I mean you harm, But these cuts I have,
C/G G F/G
and left me blind - ed by the light.
oh they need love to help them heal.
C C/B♭ Am7 Am7/G
Don't let the sun go down on me, Al-though I search my-self it's al-ways

D7/F♯
C/G
F/G
some-one else I see.
I'd just al-low a frag-ment of your life to wan-der
C
C/B♭
F/A
free,
But los-ing ev-'ry-thing is like the
Dm7
C/G
F/G
C
C/B♭
1.
F/A
C/G
sun go-ing down on me.
F/G
2.
F/A
A♭
4 fr.
B♭
6 fr.
C
8 fr.
slower

Double Vision

Words and Music by Mick Jones and Lou Gramm

Steady Rock beat
Am7
mf
D (no 3rd)
Am (no 3rd)
No chord
Am (no 3rd)
Feel-in' down and dirt-y, feel - in' kind of mean.
Nev-er do more__ than__ I real-ly need.
Am (no 3rd)
N. C.
I've been from one__ to an-oth - er ex-treme.__ It's
My mind is rac-in', but my bod-y's in the lead.__ To-

Am (no 3rd)
N. C.
time I had a good time. Ain't got time to wait.
night's the night I'm gon - na push it to the lim-it.
I
I'll
Am (no 3rd)
N. C.
want to stick a-round till I can't see straight.
live all of my years in a sin-gle min - ute.
Dm
Am
Fill my eyes with that dou - ble vi - sion.
Dm
Am
No dis-guise for that dou - ble vi - sion,

F
C
Dm
ooh,
when it gets through to me,
C/F
Dm
3
it's al-ways new to me.
1.
N.C.
My dou-ble vi-sion gets the
Am7
best of me.
C
D
2.
N.C.
My dou-ble vi-sion al-ways

Am7
seems to get the best of me,
the best of me,
yeah.
N.C.
Repeat and fade
Dm
Am
Ooh, double vision.
Repeat and fade
Dm
Am
Ooh, double vision.
N.C.

Feelings (¿Dime?)

English Words and Music by Morris Albert and Louis Gaste
Spanish Words by Thomas Fundora

Em/C♯
Cmaj7
D7
try- ing to for- get my
Tra - to de ol- vi - dar mis
feel-ings of
su- fri- mien- tos de a -
G
E7-9
C
Am7
D7
love.
mor.
Feel - ings,
¿Di - me?
for all my life I'll
si siem-pre yo a -
Bm7
E7
Am
Am7
feel it
sí - te a-mé,
I wish I'd nev- er
¿Por-qué a- ho - ra sé lo
met you, girl
ton to que fuí?
D7
Gmaj7
E7-9
Cmaj7
you'll nev- er come a - gain.
Ja - más tú vol- ve - rás.
Feel - ings,
¿Di - me?

Am7 D7 Bm7 E7 Am7 D7
wo wo wo Feel - ings, wo wo wo Feel you a-gain in my
wo wo wo, ¿Di - me? wo wo wo, ¿Di - me? A-qui en mis
R. H.
2nd time fade here
F♯m7 B9 B7-9 Em Em/D♯
arms. Feel-ings, feel-ings like I've
bra - zos. ¿Di - me? Es que
Em/D Em/C♯ Cmaj7
nev - er lost you, And feel-ings like I'll nev - er have you
pien-so que ya te he per-di-do, y Pre-sien-to que sin tí mi vi-da no
D7 G E7-9
a-gain in my heart.
no tie-ne rá - zón.
D.S. and fade on chorus

The First Time Ever I Saw Your Face

Words and Music by Ewan MacColl

Em
F
3
in your eyes
in my hand,
close to mine,
and the moon
like the trem-
and I knew
C/G
Dm7/G
C
and the stars
bling heart
our joy
were the gifts you gave
of a cap - tive bird
would fill the earth
B♭
to the dark
that was there
and last
and the end of the
at my com-
till the end of
1. C
2. C
skies.
mand my love.

3.
C
Dm7
time, my love.
The first time
C
G7
ev-er I saw your
C
B♭
C
face your face your face
B♭
C
your face.

Fire And Rain

Words and Music by James Taylor

C
Gm7
F
C
I walked out this morn - ing and I wrote down this song
My bod - y's ach - ing and my time is at hand
G
B♭maj7
I just can't re - mem - ber who to send it to.
And I won't make it an - y oth - er way.
Chorus:
F
F/E
Dm7
G7
C
I've seen fire and I've seen rain I've seen

F
F/E
Dm7
G7
C
sun-ny days_ that I thought_ would nev-er end_
I've seen
F
F/E
Dm7
G7
C
lone-ly times_ when I could not find a friend_
But I
B♭
F/A
Gm7
C9
al-ways thought that I'd see you a-gain.___
1,2
C9
2nd time to Verse 3
2. Won't you
3. Now I'm
Fine
C9

Verse 3:
C
Gm7/C
F/C
C
walk-ing my mind to an eas-y time my back turned towards the sun
G/C
B♭/C
Lord knows when the cold wind blows it-'ll turn your head a-round Well, there's
C
Gm7/C
F/C
C
hours of time on the tel-e-phone line to talk a-bout things to come
G/C
B♭/C
D.S. al Fine
Sweet dreams and fly-ing ma-chines in pie-ces on the ground.

FM

Words and Music by Walter Becker and Donald Fagen

Cmaj7
Kick off your high - heeled sneak - ers; it's par - ty time. The girls
Feed her some hun - gry reg - gae, she'll love you twice. The girls
Bm7
Am7
Em/G
F#7
B7
don't seem to care what's on, as
don't seem to care to - night, as
1.
E6/9
A13
2 fr
Bmaj7
Am7
Em7
long as they play till dawn Noth-ing but blues and El - vis and
C#m7♭5
C13
F#m/B
B7#5
2., 3.
E6/9
G#7 #9 #5
4 fr
G#m7/C#
F#9
3 fr
some-bod - y else - 's fa - v'rite song. long as the mood is right.

F#7sus4
A9
Em9
No stat - ic at all.
No stat - ic, no stat - ic at all.
F -
To Coda
C9
B+
Em7
M. No stat - ic at all.
Cmaj7
Bm7
Am7
Em/G
F#7
F
D.S. (take 2nd ending) al Coda
Coda
Em7
Em7
Repeat and fade

Garden Party

Words and Music by Rick Nelson

Moderate rock

1. I

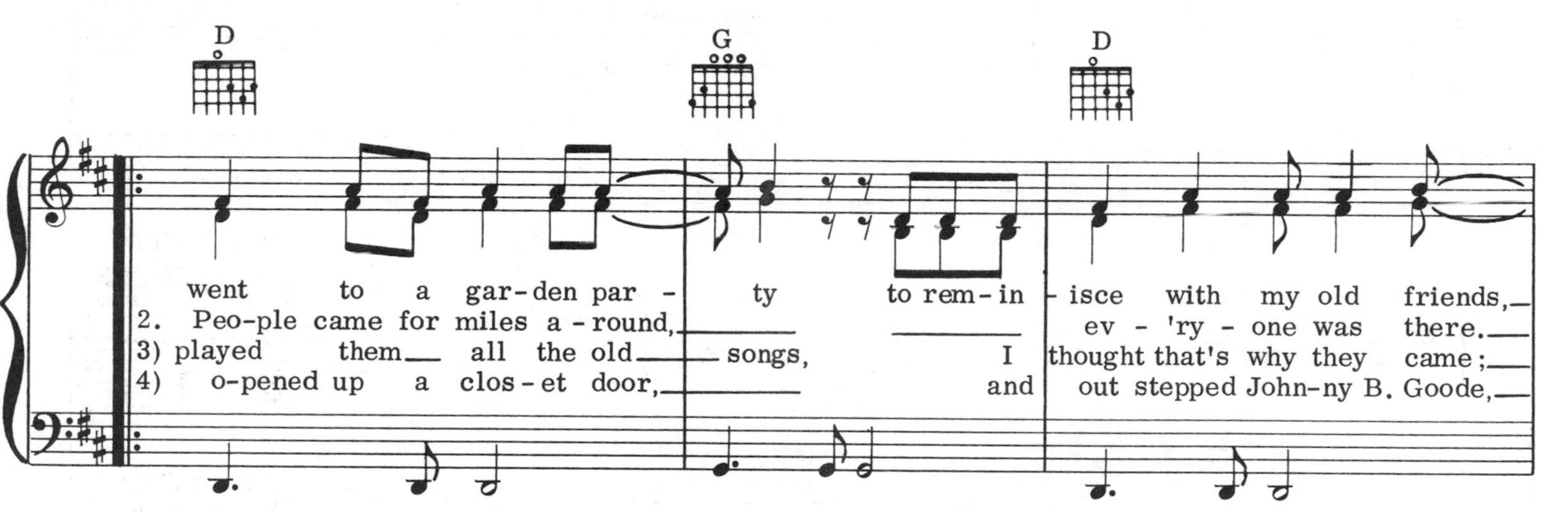
D
G
D
went to a gar-den par - ty to rem-in - isce with my old friends,
2. Peo-ple came for miles a-round, ev - 'ry - one was there.
3) played them all the old songs, I thought that's why they came;
4) o-pened up a clos-et door, and out stepped John-ny B. Goode,

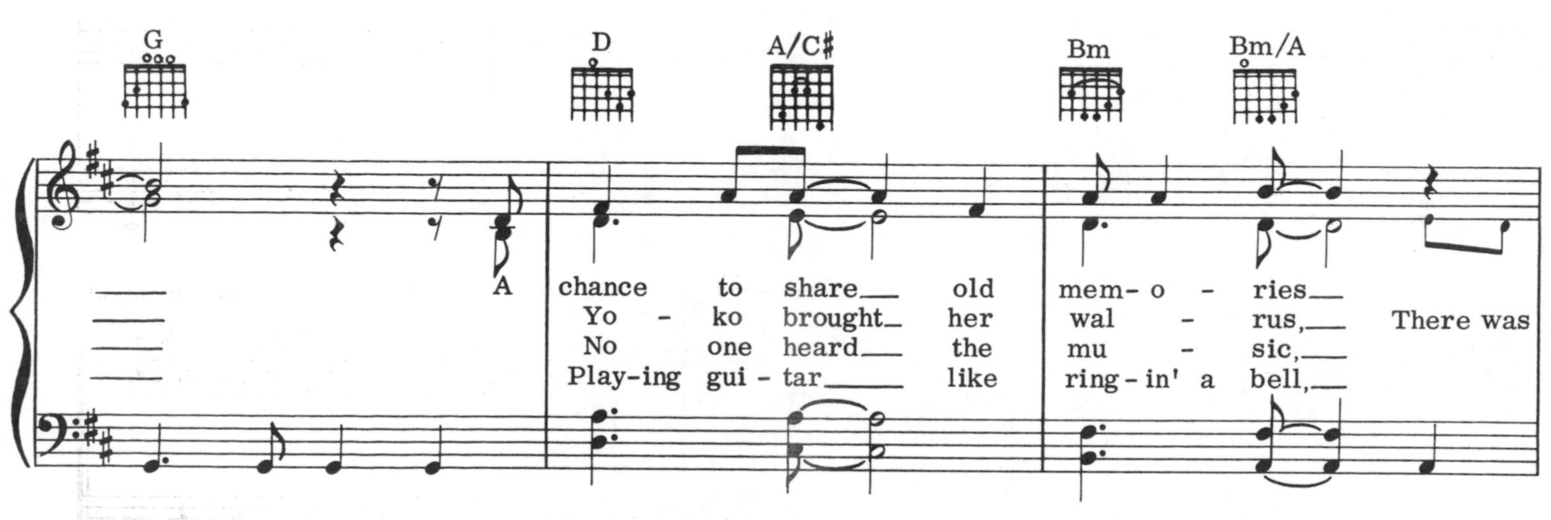
G
D
A/C#
Bm
Bm/A
A
chance to share old mem- o - ries
Yo - ko brought her wal - rus, There was
No one heard the mu - sic,
Play-ing gui - tar like ring-in' a bell,

G6 G6/A D
and play our songs a - gain. When I got to the gar - den par -
magic in the air. And o - ver in the cor -
We did-n't look the same. I said hel - lo to "Mar -
and look-in' like he should. If you got-ta play at gar - den par -
G D G
- ty, they all knew my name, But
- ner much to my sur - prise,
- y Lou," she be - longs to me, When I
- ties, I wish you a lot of luck, But if
D G
no one re - cog - nized me,
Mis - ter Hughes hid in Dy - lan's shoes,
sang a song 'bout a hon - ky - tonk,
mem - o - ries were all I sang,
Em7 Em7/A D
I did - n't look the same.
wear - ing his dis - guise.
it was time to leave.
I'd rath - er drive a truck.
But it's

Chorus
G
A
D
G
A
D
al - right now, I learned my les-son well.
G
D
You see, you can't please ev - 'ry-one, so you
Em7
Em7/A
1. D
got to please your - self.
2. D
3. I
3. D
4. Some-one
4. D
D. S. and fade
But it's

Here You Come Again

Words by Cynthia Weil
Music by Barry Mann

Abm9 (Db Bass) Db7 Abm7 (Db Bass) Db7 Bm7 Bm7 (E Bass) Amaj7 A
came to doubt you. All you got-ta do is smile that smile and
cresc.
f
Em7 (A Bass) Dmaj7 D C#m7 F#m7 F#m7 (B Bass)
there go all my de - fens-es. Just leave it up to you and in a lit -
E B (D# Bass) C#m7 F#9 F#m7 (B Bass)
tle while you're mess-in' up my mind and fill - in' up my sens-es.
G Gmaj7 (B Bass) C G Gmaj7 (B Bass)
Here you come a - gain look-in' bet - ter than a bod - y
(2nd time instrumental
mf

C
Em7
Am7
Em7
Am7
has a right to; and shak-in' me up so that all I real-ly know is
Am7
(D Bass)
1.
2. Am9
(D Bass)
D7
C
(D Bass)
D7
here you come a-gain and here I go.
cresc.
Cm7
Cm7
(F Bass)
Bbmaj7
Bb
Fm7
(Bb Bass)
All you got-ta do is smile that smile and there go all my de-
Ebmaj7
Eb
Dm7
Gm7
Gm7
(C Bass)
F
C
(E Bass)
Dm7
Dm7
(C Bass)
fens-es. Just leave it up to you and in a lit-tle while you're

G9
Gm7
(C Bass)
Ab
Abmaj7
(C Bass)
mess-in' up my mind and fill-in' up my sens-es. Here you come a - gain,
mf
Db
Ab
Abmaj7
(C Bass)
Db
look-in' bet - ter than a bod-y has a right to and
Fm7
Bbm7
Fm7
Bbm7
Bbm7
(Eb Bass)
shak-in' me up so that all I real-ly know is here you come a - gain
Ab
Abmaj7
(C Bass)
Db
Repeat and fade
and here I go here I go
f
mf

From the Motion Picture SATURDAY NIGHT FEVER

How Deep Is Your Love

Words and Music by Barry Gibb, Maurice Gibb and Robin Gibb

A♭maj7
Gm7
3 fr
to me on a sum - mer breeze, keep me warm
not think I care for you when you know
Fm7
D♭9
in your love, then you soft - ly leave.
down in - side that I real - ly do.
And it's
Gm7
3 fr
A♭/B♭
how deep is your love?
E♭
3 fr
me you need to show;
how deep is your love? How deep
E♭maj7
3 fr
A♭maj7
A♭m6
4 fr
is your love?
I real - ly mean to learn.
'Cause we're

E♭
B♭m/D♭
C7
liv - ing in a world of fools, breaking us down when they all
Fm7
A♭m6
should let us be. We be - long to you and me.
E♭
Gm7
A♭/B♭
D.S. and Fade
How deep
Optional Ending
E♭
E♭maj7
E♭
is your love? How deep is your love?

I Just Want To Be Your Everything

Words and Music by Barry Gibb

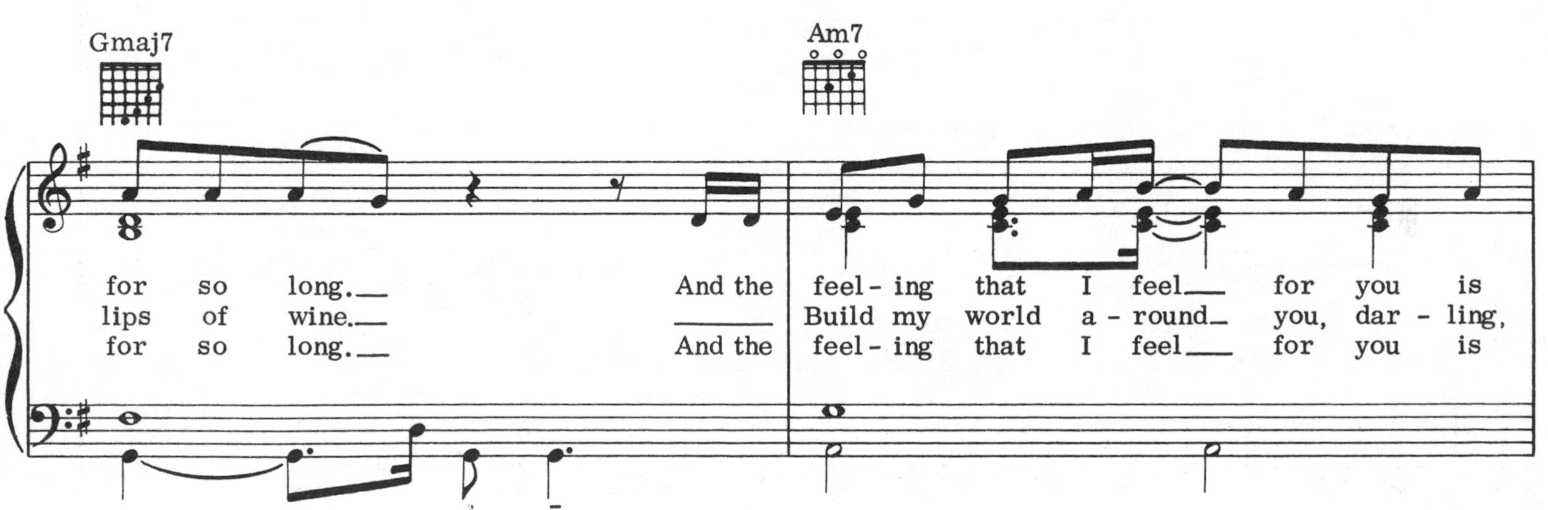

Cmaj7
G
Em
more than strong, girl,
take it from me.
If you
this love will shine, girl,
watch it and see.
If you
more than strong, girl,
watch it and see.
If you
1. Am7
Am7/D
give a lit-tle more than you're ask-ing for, your
love will turn the key.
Dar-ling
2. 3.
Am7
Am7/D
give a lit-tle more than you're ask-ing for, your
love will turn the key.
Chorus
Cmaj7
D7
I,
I just want to be your ev-'ry-
Oh,
If I stay here with-out you, dar-ling,

Gmaj7
E7
thing.
I will die.
O - pen up the heav - en in your
I want you lay - ing in the
Am7
Am7/D
D7
(Add small notes 2nd time)
heart and let me be the things you are to me, and not some
love I have to bring... I'd do an - y - thing to be your
1. Gmaj7
G+
pup - pet on a string.
2. G
G+
D. C. and fade on Chorus
ev - 'ry - thing.

I Can See Clearly Now

Words and Music by Johnny Nash

F
C
G
bright, bright sun-shin-y day,
It's gon-na be a
F
C
G
Last time D. S. and fade
bright, bright sun-shin-y day.
B♭
F
Look all a- round there's noth-ing but blue sky,
B♭
D
D. C.
Look straight a- head, noth-ing but blue sky.

I Write The Songs

Words and Music by Bruce Johnston

F
Fmaj7
Gm7
C7
Gm7
C7
I write the songs that make the whole world sing; I write the songs of love and
F
Am7/E
Dm
Dm(♯7)
Dm7
spe - cial things. I write the songs that make the
G7sus
G7
Gm7/C
young girls cry; I write the songs, I write the songs.
Melody
1. 3.
F
B♭m/F
F
Fine, last time end here
2.
F
Oh, my

E7sus
E7
Em7
E7
mu - sic makes you dance and gives you spir - it to take a chance,
A
A/G♯
F♯m
A/E
And I wrote some rock 'n' roll so you can move.
G7sus
G7
G7sus
G7
Mu - sic fills your heart, well, that's a real fine place to start, It's from me
Gm7/C
C
Gm7/C
C
Gm7/C
C
Gm7/C
C
D. S. al Fine
it's for you, it's from you, it's for me, it's a world wide sym - pho-ny.
cresc.

It Never Rains (In Southern California)

Words and Music by Albert Hammond and Michael Hazelwood

Moderately
f
Am7
D
G
𝄋
Got on board a west - bound sev-en for-ty sev - en,
Will you tell the folks back home I near-ly made it,
mf
Am7
D
G
C
Did-n't think be-fore de-cid - ing what to do.
Had of - fers but don't know which one to take.
G
Am7
D
G
All that talk of op - por-tu - ni-ties T. V. breaks and mov -
Please don't tell them how you found me Don't tell them how you found

Am7
D
G
C
G
- ies rang true, sure rang true.
me give me a break give me a break.
Am7
D
G
Seems it nev - er rains in South - ern Cal - i - for - nia
Am7
D
G
Seems I've of - ten heard that kind of talk be - fore.
Am7
D
G
It nev - er rains in Cal - i - for - nia, But girl, don't they warn

Em
Am7
D
G
C
G
Fine
ya, It pours, man, it pours.
Am7
D
G
Out of work, I'm out a' my head, Out of self-re- spect, I'm out a' bread.
Am7
D
G
I'm un - der - loved, I'm un - der - fed. I wan-na go home.
Am7
D
G
It nev - er rains in Cal - i - for - nia, But girl, don't they warn
Em
Am7
D
G
C
G
D. S. al Fine
ya, It pours, man, it pours.

Imagine

Words and Music by John Lennon

Slowly
C
Cmaj7
F
mf
I-mag-ine there's no heav-en.
It's eas - y if you try.
No hell below us,
a-bove us on - ly sky.

Am/E
Dm7
F/C
G
C/G
I-mag-ine all the peo-ple liv-ing for to-day.
G7
C
Cmaj7
F
Ah.
I-mag-ine there's no coun-tries.
sions.
C
Cmaj7
F
It is-n't hard to do.
I won-der if you can.
C
Cmaj7
F
Noth-ing to kill or die for,
No need for greed or hun-ger,

C
Cmaj7
F
and no re - li - gion, too.
a broth - er - hood of man.
Am/E
Dm7
F/C
G
C/G
I-mag-ine all the peo - ple liv - ing life in peace.
I-mag-ine all the peo - ple shar - ing all the world.
G7
F
G
You, you may say I'm a
C
E7
F
G
dream - er, but I'm not the on - ly one.

C
E7
F
G
I hope some - day you'll
C
E7
1
F
G
join us
and the world will
C
Cmaj7
be as one.
I - mag - ine no pos - ses -
2
F
G
C
and the world will live as one.
rit.

Island Girl

Words and Music by Elton John and Bernie Taupin

Moderato
gliss.
f
gliss.
Dm
Bb/F
I see your teeth flash, Ja- mai - can hon - ey so sweet,
mp - mf
C/G
F/A
Bb
down where Lex - ing - ton cross for - ty sev - enth street.
Dm
Oh, she's a big girl, she's stand - ing six foot three,

B♭/F
F
turn-ing tricks for the dudes in the
C/G
A♭
4 fr.
E♭
3 fr.
big cit - y.
Is - land
B♭
F
girl, what you want - in' wid de white man's world?
E♭
3 fr.
B♭
Is - land girl, black boy want you in his is - land
F
B♭
world. He want to take you from de

Bb/A
Bb/Ab
3 fr.
Eb
3 fr.
rack-et boss, He want to save you but de cause is lost.
Bb
Bb7
Eb
3 fr.
C7
Is - land girl, is - land girl, is - land girl,
Bb/F
Eb/G
F7/A
Bb
N. C.
tell me what you want-in' wid de white man's world.
gliss.
F
Bb
F
Bb
gliss.
She's
(Instrumental 2nd time)

Dm
B♭/F
black as coal
but she burn like a fire
C/G
F/A
And she wrap her-self a-round you
like a well-worn tire.
B♭
Dm
You feel her nail scratch your back just like a rake,
B♭/F
F
Oh, he one more gone, he one
C/G
A♭
4 fr.
1.
E♭
3 fr.
2.
A♭
4 fr.
E♭
3 fr.
D. S. and fade
more john who make de mis-take.
Is-land
Is - land

It's Too Late

Words by Toni Stern
Music by Carole King

D♭maj7
Fmaj7
B♭maj7
Fmaj7
real-ly did try to make it.
Some-thin' in-side has died and I can't hide
1.2.
Dm7
Fmaj7
E7sus
Em7
Am7
D6
Am7
And I just can't fake it.
D6
3.
Dm7
Fmaj7
G7sus
G7
Cmaj7
2. It
3.
And I just can't fake it.
It's too late, ba-
Fmaj7
Cmaj7
Fmaj7
Cmaj7
-by, It's too late now, dar-lin', It's too late.

From SATURDAY NIGHT FEVER

Jive Talkin'

Words and Music by Barry Gibb, Maurice Gibb and Robin Gibb

F
C
gets in my eyes.
wear a dis - guise.
is - n't a crime. And if there's
No - bod - y be -
Jive talk - in', so
some - bod - y you'll
B♭
C
To Coda
After repeat
D. S. al Coda
lieves what you say; it's just your
mis - un - der - stood, yeah;
love till you die, then all that
jive talk - in' that
jive talk - in', you
jive talk - in', just
gets in the way.
just ain't no good.
Coda
B♭
C
N. C.
1. 2. 3.
gets in your eye.
4.
C
Repeat and fade
do doot do.
Jive talk - in'.

Just The Way You Are

Words and Music by Billy Joel

Bm7/E
E9
G/A
And I don't see you any-more
Al-though I might not seem to care
I
I
D
Bm6
Gmaj7
Bm
D7
would not leave you in times of trou-ble
don't want clev-er con-ver-sa-tion
said I love you and that's for-ev-er
Gmaj7
Gm
D/F#
Am7
D7
We nev-er could have come this far mm mm
I nev-er want to work that hard mm mm
And this I prom-ise from the heart mm mm
Gmaj7
Gm
D/F#
Bm7
I took the good times I'll take the bad times
I just want some-one that I can talk to
I could not love you an-y bet-ter

Em7
G/A
Last time to Coda
D
Gm6/D
D
G/D
D
I'll take you just the way you are.
I want you just the way you are.
I love you just the way you are.
1.
Gm6/D
D
G/D
D
2.
Gm6/D
D
D7
G
A
F♯m7
B7
I need to know that you will al - ways be
Em7
A
D
Am/C
The same old some - one that I knew
Oh,

B♭
C
Am7
D
D7
what will it take till you be - lieve in me
Gm7
C
G/A
D. S. al Coda
The way that I believe in you And I
Coda
B♭
C
Am7
D7
Gm7
A7
Dmaj7
melody
Whoa.

Killing Me Softly With His Song

Words by Norman Gimbel
Music by Charles Fox

Dm7
G
And there he was this young boy
I prayed that he would fin - ish
But he was there this stran - ger
C
E7
a stran - ger to my eyes.
but he just kept right on.
sing - ing clear and strong.
Am
F
Strum - ming my pain with his fin - gers,
G
C
Sing - ing my life with his words.

Am
D/F♯
G
Kill-ing me soft - ly with his song, Kill-ing me soft - ly with his
F
C
song Tell-ing my whole life with his
F
B♭
words, Kill-ing me soft - ly with his song.
1. 2.
A
3.
A
G/A
A

Tuner functions

TUNER ON/OFF SWITCH

Power is turned on or off by each press of this switch. The tuner will turn off automatically after 5 minutes. (You can turn this on even if no cable is connected.)

A protection circuit will operate immediately after the power is turned on, so the tuner may not respond to a softly-played note. Play the first note strongly in order to activate the tuner.

NOTE INDICATOR LEDs

These LEDs indicate the note of the strings you are playing. When tuning sharp or flat notes such as G#, both the G indicator and the # indicator will light up. If the note shown on the note indicator LED is different from the one you wish, try tightening or loosening the string until the correct LED lights up. Be careful not to tighten the strings too much (over tune) as the strings may break. When in doubt, it is better to tune down and loosen the strings and then tune back up to find the desired pitch.

TUNING GUIDE LEDs

When the string is in tune, the green LED in the middle will light up. If the pitch of the string is flat, the red LED on the left will light up. If the pitch of the string is sharp, the red LED on the right will light.

Notes

Replace the batteries if you notice any of the following things.

- Decreased sound quality or volume
- The tuner does not respond when you turn it on
- The LEDs do not operate when you turn on the tuner
- The battery check LED is lit or blinking

To prevent the battery from being consumed needlessly, disconnect the plug from the output jack when you're not using the guitar.

(Fishman, Sonicore and PREFIX PLUS-T are trademarks of Fishman Tranducers Inc.

Last Dance

Words and Music by Paul Jabara

D♭/E♭
E♭7
A♭maj7
4fr.
night.
Oh,
I
need
you
by
B♭/A♭
Gm7
3fr.
Cm7
3fr.
me,
be - side
me,
to guide
me,
to
A♭maj7
4fr.
B♭/A♭
G7sus4
3fr.
G7
3fr.
hold
me,
to scold
me,
'cause when I'm bad,
I'm
so,
so
bad.
Cm7
3fr.
F7
E♭/B♭
6fr.
A♭/B♭
4fr.
So
let's
dance
the
last
dance.

Eb/Bb
6fr.
Ab/Bb
4fr.
Eb/Bb
6fr.
Let's dance the last dance. Let's dance this
Ab/Bb
4fr.
1.
Am7b5
4fr.
Abmaj7/Bb
last dance to - night.
2.
Am7b5
4fr.
Abmaj7
4fr.
Eb/G
night.
Fm7
Ab/Bb
4fr.
Eb
6fr.

Knock Three Times

Words and Music by Irwin Levine and L. Russell Brown

Moderately

Verse

D
Hey, girl, what-cha do - in' down there? Danc-in' a-lone ev-'ry night while I live right a-
you look out your win - dow to-night, Pull in the string with the note that's at-tached to my

A7
bove you. I can hear your mu - sic play - in',
heart. Read how man - y times I saw you, How

I can feel your bod - y sway - in', One floor be - low me, you
in my si - lence I a - dore you, And on - ly in my dreams did

Chorus
D
G
A7
D7
Dmaj7
don't e-ven know me, I love_you.
that wall be-tween us come a-part,
Oh, my dar-lin', Knock Three Times on the ceil-ing if you
want_ me;_
Twice on the pipe
if the an-swer is
no.
Oh, my sweet-ness, (Knock) means you'll meet me in the
hall-way;_
Twice on the pipe
means you ain't gon-na show.
2. If
Oh, my dar-lin',
D.S. and fade

Knockin' On Heaven's Door

Music and Lyrics by Bob Dylan

G
D
Am7
mf
Knock, knock, knock-in' on heav-en's door
G
D
C
Knock, knock, knock-in' on heav-en's door
G
D
Am7
Knock, knock, knock-in' on heav-en's door
G
D
1. C
2. C
Knock, knock, knock-in' on heav-en's door
G
D
Am7
Repeat and fade
mp
With pedal

Layla

Words and Music by Eric Clapton and Jim Gordon

Moderately
f
C♯m
4 fr.
G♯m
4 fr.
What will you do when you get lone - ly
Tried to give you con - so - la - tion,
Let's make the best of the situ - a - tion,

C♯m
4 fr.
D
E
with no-bod-y wait - ing by your side?
your old man won't let you down.
be - fore I fin - 'ly go in - sane.
8 bassa-
F♯m7
A/B
E
A
You've been run-ning and hid - ing much too long,
Like a fool I fell in love with you,
Please don't say we'll nev - er find a way
F♯m7
B
E
A
you know it's just your fool - ish pride.
turned the whole world up - side down.
and tell me all my love's in vain.
Lay -
Dm
B♭
C
Dm
B♭
la, you got me on my knees. Lay - la, I'm

C
Dm
Bb
C
Dm
beg-ging, dar-ling, please. Lay - la,
Dar-ling, won't you ease my wor-ried
Bb
1. 2.
C
3.
C
Dm
mind.
Lay -
Dm
Bb
C
Dm
la,
you
got me on my knees. Lay -
Bb
C
Dm
Repeat and fade
la,
I'm
beg-ging, dar - ling, please. Lay -

Let It Be

Words and Music by John Lennon and Paul McCartney

Am G F C G
standing right in front of me speaking words of wisdom; let it
F C/E Dm7 C G/B Am G
be. Let it be, let it be, let it be,
Instrumental ends Let it be, let it be, let it be,
F C G
let it be. Whisper words of wisdom; let it be.
let it be. Whisper words of wisdom; let it be.
F C/E Dm7 C G
And when the broken-hearted people
And when the night is cloudy, there is

Am G F C G
liv - ing in the world a - gree there will be an an - swer, let it
still a light that shines on me. Shine un - til to - mor - row; let it
F C/E Dm7 C G
be. For though they may be part - ed, there is
be. I wake up to the sound of mu - sic,
Am G F C G
still a chance that they will see there will be an an - swer; let it
Moth - er Mar - y comes to me speak - ing words of wis - dom; let it
F C/E Dm7 C G/B Am G
be.
be.
Let it be, let it be, let it be,

F C G
let it be. There will be an an - swer; let it be.
F C/E Dm7 C G/B Am G
Let it be, let it be, let it be,
F C G
To Coda
let it be.
Whis - per words of wis - dom; let it be.
There will be an an - swer; let it be.
F C/E Dm7 C F Em Dm7 C B♭ F/A

G
F
C
F
C
G
F
C
D.S. al Coda
CODA
F
C/E
Dm7
C
G/B
Am
G
Let it be, let it be, let it be,
F
C
G
let it be. Whis-per words of wis - dom; let it be.
F
C/E
Dm7
C
F
Em
Dm7
C
B♭
F/A
G
F
C

Let Your Love Flow

Words and Music by Larry E. Williams

F/G
C
So let that feel - ing grab you
So let the won - der take you
F/G
C
deep in - side and send you reel - ing where your
in - to space and lay you un - der its
F/G
G7
love can't hide and then go steal - ing through the
lov - ing em - brace Feel the thun - der as it
C
sum - mer nights with your love - er.
warms your face; you can't hold back.

C7
F
(Just) let your
love
flow
like a
moun- tain
stream; (and)
let your
C
love
grow
with the
small - est
of
dreams
and
let
your
G7
love
show.
And you'll
know
what
I
mean;
it's
the
sea-
C
- son.
C7
F
Let your
love
fly
like a

C
bird on the wing. (And) let your
love bind you to all
G7
living things, and let your
love shine and you'll
1.
C
know what I mean, that's the rea-
son.
F/G
2. There's a
2.
C
son.
C7
D. S. and fade
Let your

Love So Right

Words and Music by Barry Gibb, Maurice Gibb and Robin Gibb

Amaj7
G♯m7
4 fr.
F♯m7
Emaj7
lov-ing me. And I thought I'd found the heav-en in her eyes. But the
close to me? And the per-fect sto-ry end-ed at the start. I
F♯m7
B7
G♯7
4 fr.
C♯m
4 fr.
morn-ing when I woke up, I was here and she was gone;
thought you came for-ev-er, and you came to break my heart.
now I'm
F♯m7
F♯m7/B
hang-ing on.
May-be you can tell me how a
On the chance that you'll come back to me? How a
cresc.
Amaj7
G♯m7
4 fr.
C♯m7
4 fr.
F♯m7
love so right can turn out to be so wrong, oh, my dar-
mf

F♯m7/B
Amaj7
G♯m7
4 fr.
C♯m7
4 fr.
To Coda
- ling. How a love so right can turn out to be so wrong.
F♯m7
F♯m7/B
E
F♯m7
D. S. al Coda
Where did she go when I need her
mp
Coda
F♯m7
F♯m7/B
A
oh, my dar - ling. I could take it in my stride, start
Am
G♯m7
4 fr.
liv - ing for the mo - ment. May-be half the things we sought were

C♯7
4 fr.
F♯m7
nev - er there. Sim - ply o - pen up our eyes and
F♯m7/B
break it down to size. It is - n't real - ly fair how a
Amaj7
G♯m7
4 fr.
C♯m7
4 fr.
love so right can turn out to be so wrong,
F♯m7
F♯m7/B
Repeat and fade
oh, my dar - ling. How a

Maggie May

Words and Music by Rod Stewart and Martin Quittenton

Am
Bm
Am7
Mag-gie, I could-n't have tried any more. You
Am
D
Am
lured me a-way from home, just to save you from be-ing a-lone.
lured me a-way from home, just to save you from be-ing a-lone.
lured me a-way from home, 'cause you did-n't want to be a-lone.
D
Am
D
G
You stole my heart and that's what real-ly hurts.
You stole my soul that's a pain I can do with-out.
You stole my heart I could-n't leave you if I tried.
D
C
The morn-ing sun, when it's in your face real-ly
All I needed was a friend to lend a
I sup-pose I could col-lect my books and get

G
D
shows your age. But that don't wor - ry me
guid - ing hand. But you turned in - to a lov - er and
back to school. Or steal my dad - dy's cue and
C
G
none; in my eyes you're ev - 'ry - thing. I
Moth - er, what a lover you wore me out. All you
make a liv - ing out of play - ing pool. Or
C
G
C
laughed at all of your jokes, my love you did - n't need to coax,
did was wreck my bed, And in the morn - ing kick me in the head,
find my - self a rock and roll band that needs a help - ing hand,
D
Am
Bm
Oh, Mag - gie, I could - n't have tried an - y
Oh, Mag - gie, I could - n't have tried an - y
Oh, Mag - gie, I wish I'd nev - er seen your

1.2.
Am
Bm
3.
more.
more.
2. You
3. You
face.
You made a
D
C7
G
first class fool out of me,
But I'm as
blind as a fool can be,
You
stole my heart but I
love you an - y - way.
C
Repeat and fade
(shouted) Maggie, I wish I'd never seen your face.
get on back home one of these days.
I'll

Mandy

Words and Music by Scott English and Richard Kerr

Cm
1
Eb/Bb
Ab
Shad-ows of a man, a face through a win-dow, cry-in' in the night, the
Look-ing in their eyes, I
Caught up in a world of
Eb/F
2,3
Eb/Bb
Ab
night goes in - to
see a mem - r'y. I nev-er re-al-ized how
up - hill climb - ing, the tears are in my mind and
Eb/F
Bb
Gm
Eb
hap-py you made me.
noth-in' is rhym - ing.
Oh, Man - dy, well you came and you gave with-out tak -
F
Eb/F
Bb
- ing, but I sent you a-way. Oh, Man - dy, well you kissed

Gm
Eb
F
Eb/F
To Coda
me and stopped me from shak - ing,
and I need you to - day. Oh,
Bb
Gm7
Eb
F11
D.S. al Coda
(take 2nd ending)
Man - dy!
I'm
CODA
Gm
Dm
Eb
Man - dy!
Cm9
Fsus
F7
Cm
Yes-ter-day's a dream, I

Eb/Bb
6 fr
Ab
4 fr
Eb/F
face the morn - ing, cry - ing on a breeze, the pain is call - ing. Oh, Man -
Bb
Gm
3 fr
Eb
3 fr
F
- dy, well you came and you gave with - out tak - ing, but I
Eb/F
Bb
Gm
3 fr
Eb
3 fr
sent you a - way. Oh, Man - dy, well you kissed me and stopped me from shak -
F
Eb/F
C
- ing, and I need you to - day. Oh, Man - dy, well you came

Am
F
G
G7sus
and you gave with-out tak - ing, but I sent you a - way. Oh, Man -
C
Am
F
G
dy, well you kissed me and stopped me from shak - ing, and I
G7sus
C
Am
F
need you.
(Vocal 1st time only)
Repeat and Fade
Optional Ending
G
F/G
C

Misty Blue

Words and Music by Bob Montgomery

G
B♭
C
E♭
looks like I'd get you off of my mind,
C+
E♭+
Dm7
Fm7
but I can't
Just the thought of you
G
B♭
C
E♭
turns my whole world mist - y blue.
C
E♭
C+
E♭+
Dm7
Fm7
Oh hon - ey,
just the men - tion of your name

G
B♭
C
E♭
turns the flick - er to a flame. Lis - ten
C +
E♭+
Dm7
Fm7
to me good, ba - by. I think of the things we used to do,
G
B♭
C
E♭
and my whole world turns mist - y blue.
C
E♭
C +
E♭+
Dm7
Fm7
Oh, ba - by, I should for - get

G
B♭
C
E♭
you. Heav-en knows, I've tried.
cresc.
Em
Gm
F
A♭
Ba-by, when I say that I'm glad we're through,
f
G
B♭
C
E♭
deep in my heart I know I've lied, I've lied,
C+
E♭+
Dm7
Fm7
I've lied. (Just the thought of you,
mf

G
B♭
C
E♭
mist - y blue.)
C
E♭
C+
E♭+
Dm7
Fm7
Oh hon - ey, it's been such a long, long time,
G
B♭
C
E♭
looks like I'd get you off of my mind,
C+
E♭+
Dm7
Fm7
but I can't. Just the thought of you, my love,

G
B♭
C
E♭
my whole world turns mist - y blue.
cresc.
C
C+
Dm7
E♭
E♭+
Fm7
Oh,
oh, I can't, oh, I can't, oh, I can't for -
f
G
B♭
C
E♭
get you. My whole world turns mist - y blue.
C+
Dm7
E♭+
Fm7
Oh,
oh, my love,

G
B♭
C
E♭
my whole world turns mist - y blue.
C
E♭
C+
E♭+
Dm7
Fm7
Ba - by, ba - by, ba - by, ba - by, ba - by, I can't for - get you.
G
B♭
C
E♭
Repeat and fade
My whole world turns mist - y blue.

My Love

Words and Music by McCartney

1.
2. 3.
B♭
F
My love does it good.
Wo - wo
mf
Gm7
C7
F+/A
Last time to Coda
I love, oh wo, my love, On - ly
my love holds the oth - er key to me, Oh wo
My love, oh my love, on - ly

B♭ C7 F Dm/B
my love does it good to me. Wo - wo
F Gm7 B♭
wo - wo, wo - wo - wo - wo, My love does it good.
F
D. S. al Coda
Coda
Gm7/B♭ C7
My love does it good to
F F+/A B♭ C13 F
me. Wo wo wo wo wo wo wo.

Never Can Say Goodbye

Words and Music by Clifton Davis

Dmaj7
Am7/D
tried and tried to hide my feel - ings, they al - ways seem to show. Then you
ver - y strange vi - bra - tion pierc - ing me right to the core. It says,
same un - hap - py feel - ing that there's that an - guish, there's that doubt. It's the
Dmaj7
Am7/D
try to say you're leav - ing me, and I al - ways have to say, "No, tell me
"Turn a - round, you fool. You know you love her more and more." Tell me
same old diz - zy hang - up; can't do with you or with - out. Tell me
Gmaj7
1
Em7
Em7/A
2
Em7
Em7/A
To Coda
why is it so?" But I
why is it so? Don't wan - na let you go.
why is it so?
Dmaj7
Dm7
E7/D
E♭maj7/D
D5
5 fr
I nev - er can say good - bye, girl.
I nev - er can say good - bye,

Dmaj7
Dm7
no, no, no, no, no, no, no, no, no, no, no. Oh, I nev-er can say good-bye, girl.
E7/D
E♭maj7/D
D
D.S. al Coda
I nev-er can say good-bye, no, no, no, no, no, no, no, no, no.
CODA
Em7
Em7/A
Dmaj7
Dm7
Don't wan-na let you go. I nev-er can say good-bye, girl.
E7/D
E♭maj7/D
D
Dmaj7
Repeat and Fade
I nev-er can say good-bye, no, no, no, no, no, no, no, no, no. I nev-er can say good-bye,

Nights In White Satin

Words and Music by Justin Hayward

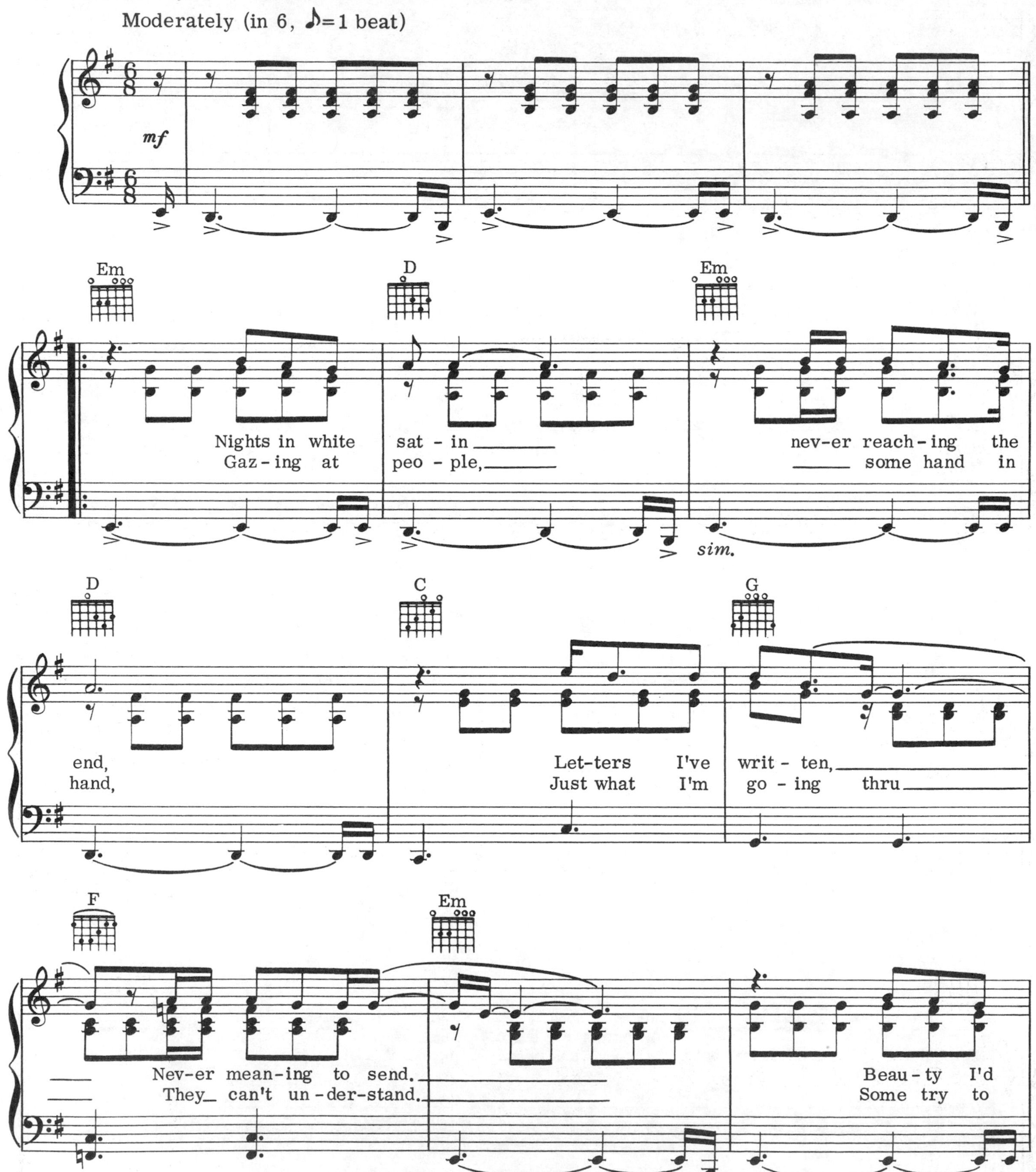

D
Em
D
C
al-ways missed with these eyes before,
Just what the
tell me thoughts they can-not de-fend,
Just what you
G
F
Em
A
truth-is
I can't say an-y-more.
'Cause I love you,
want to be,
You'll be in the end.
And I love you,
C
Em
Yes, I love you,
Oh, how I love you!
D
Em
D
Em

Nights On Broadway

Words and Music by Barry Gibb, Maurice Gibb and Robin Gibb

Moderately slow, with a strong beat
To Coda
N.C.
mf
Dm
Here we are in a room full of stran - gers,
in my place there are so man-y oth - ers
Am
Dm
stand - ing in the dark where your eyes could - n't
stand - ing in the line; how long will they stand be -

Am
see me.
tween us?
Well, I have_ to
Bb
fol - low you
Bbm
though you did_ not
F
want me to.
But that won't stop_ my
Gm
3 fr.
lov - in' you;_
I can't stay_ a -

A
F
way.
Blam-in' it all
on the nights on
cresc.
f
Am
Bb
Broad - way,
sing-in' them
love songs,
sing-in' them
Bbm
F
straight-to - the-heart songs. Blam-in' it all
on the nights on
Am
Bb
Broad - way,
sing-in' them
sweet sounds
to that

1.
B♭m
2.
B♭m
D. C. al Coda
cra - zy, cra - zy town. Now
cra - zy, cra - zy town,
mf
Coda
N. C.
Am
mp
I will wait,
Dm
F
e - ven if it takes for -
G
Em
ev - er; I will wait,

Am
G
F
e - ven if it takes a life - time. Some - how I feel in - side
C
you nev - er ev - er left my side. Make it like it
F
Am
was be - fore e - ven if it takes a life -
Am/G
Am/D
D. S. and fade
time, takes a life - time. Blam - in' it all
cresc.
f

Raindrops Keep Fallin' On My Head

Lyric by Hal David
Music by Burt Bacharach

Fmaj7
F7
B♭
Am7
D7
sun. And I said I did-n't like the way he got things done. Sleep-in' on the
Am7
D7
Gm7
3 fr
B♭/C
C
job. Those rain-drops are fall-in' on my head. They keep fall-in'! But there's one
F
Fmaj7
B7
B♭
C
C7
thing I know The blues they send to meet me won't de-feat
Am7
D9
4 fr
me. It won't be long till hap-pi-ness steps up

Gm7
B♭/C
C
B♭/C
C
F
to greet _ me.
Rain - drops keep fall - in' on my
Fmaj7
F7
B♭
Am7
D7
head,
but that does - n't mean my eyes will soon be turn - in' red.
Cry - in's not for
Am7
D7
Gm7
me
'cause
I'm nev - er gon - na stop the rain by com - plain - in'.
B♭/C
C
F
Fmaj7
Gm7
B♭/C
F
Be - cause I'm free
noth - in's wor - ry - in' me.

Philadelphia Freedom

Words and Music by Elton John and Bernie Taupin

G7
3 fr.
But the times have changed;
The less I say the more
Fm6/Ab
3 fr.
Gm7
F
Bb
6 fr.
my work gets done.
'Cause I live and breathe this
f
F
Bb
6 fr.
Phil-a-del-phi-a free-dom.
From the day that I was born
F
I waved the flag
Eb
6 fr.
D7
3 fr.
Gm7
Phil-a-del-phia free-dom took me knee-high to a man

Eb9
6 fr.
D7
3 fr.
Db
4 fr.
Bb
6 fr.
Yeah! Gave me peace of mind_my dad - dy nev-er had.
F
Bb
6 fr.
Oh, Phil- a - del-phi-a free - dom shine on me I love
Am7
5 fr.
Gm7
Am7
5 fr.
G7/B
it. Shine the light through the eyes of the one left be-hind.
C7
Em7/A
A7
5 fr.
Dm
5 fr.
Gm7
Shine the light, shine the light.

Verse 2. If you choose to, you can live your life alone
Some people choose the city,
Some others choose the good old family home
I like living easy without family ties
'Til the whippoorwill of freedom zapped me
Right between the eyes. *(Repeat Chorus)*

Piano Man

Words and Music by Billy Joel

F C/E D7 G C
reg - u - lar crowd shuf - fles in There's an old man
gets me my drinks for free, And he's quick with a
nev - er had time for a wife And he's talk - in' with
man - ag - er gives me a smile 'Cause he knows that it's
Em/B Am C/G F G11
sit - ting next to me Mak - in' love to his ton - ic and
joke or to light up your smoke But there's some-place that he'd rath - er
Dav - y who's still in the Nav - y And prob - ab - ly will be for
me they've been com - in' to see To for get a - bout life for a
C F/C Cmaj7 G11 C
gin. He says, "Son, can you
be. He says, "Bill, I be -
life. And the wait - ress is
while. And the pia - no
mf
Em/B Am C/G F C/E
play me a mem - o - ry? I'm not real - ly sure how it
lieve this is kill-ing me," As a smile ran a - way from his
prac - tic - ing pol - i - tics, As the bus - 'ness - men slow - ly get
sounds like a car - ni - val And the mic - ro - phone smells like a

D7 G C Em/B Am
goes, But it's sad and it's sweet and I knew it com -
face "Well, I'm sure that I could be a mov - ie
stoned Yes, they're shar - ing a drink they call lone - li -
beer And they sit at the bar and put bread in my
C/G F G11 C
plete When I wore a young - er man's clothes."
star If I could get out of this place."
ness But it's bet - ter than drink - in' a - lone.
jar And say "Man, what are you do - in' here?"
Am Am/G D7/F♯ F Am
Da da da de de da da da
Da da da de de da da da
Instrumental
Da da da de de da da da
mp
Am/G D7/F♯ D7 G G/F C/E
de de da da da
de de da da da
de de da da da

G7/D
C
Em/B
Am
C/G
Sing us a song, you're the pia - no man
f
F
C/E
D7
G
C
Sing us a song to - night.
Well, we're all in the
Em/B
Am
C/G
F
G11
mood for a mel - o - dy,
And you've got us feel - in' al -
C
F/C
Cmaj7
1. 2. 3.
G11
4.
G11
D. C. al Fine
right.
2. Now
3. Now
4. It's a

Rocky Mountain High

Words by John Denver

Music by John Denver and Mike Taylor

Moderately

Guitar → *D (Capo up 2 frets) H.O. Em7 H.O. G 5 fr. H.O. A 7 fr. H.O.

Keyboard → E F#m7 A B

mp *mf*

He was born

D H.O. E Em7 H.O. (sim. throughout) F#m7

in the sum - mer of his twen-ty sev-enth
Ca-the - dral Moun - tains, he saw sil - ver clouds be-low,

C D A 7 fr. B D E Em7 F#m7

year, com-in' home to a place he'd nev-er been be-fore.
he saw ev - 'ry-thing as far as you can see.

G 5 fr. A A 7 fr. B D E

He left yes - ter-day be - hind him, you might
And they say that he got cra - zy once and he

*Guitarists: Tune low E down to D.

Em7
C
A
7 fr.
D
F♯m7
D
B
E
say he was born a - gain, you might say he found a key
tried to touch the sun, and he lost a friend but
Em7
G
5 fr.
A
7 fr.
F♯m7
A
B
for ev - 'ry door When he
kept his mem - o - ry. Now he
(Now his
D
E
Em7
F♯m7
first came to the moun - tains his life was far a - way,
walks in qui-et sol - i - tude, the for - ests and the streams
life) is full of won - der but his heart still knows some fear
C
A
7 fr.
D
Em7
D
B
E
F♯m7
on the road and hang - in' by a song.
seek-ing grace in ev - 'ry step he takes.
of a sim - ple thing he can - not com - pre - hend.

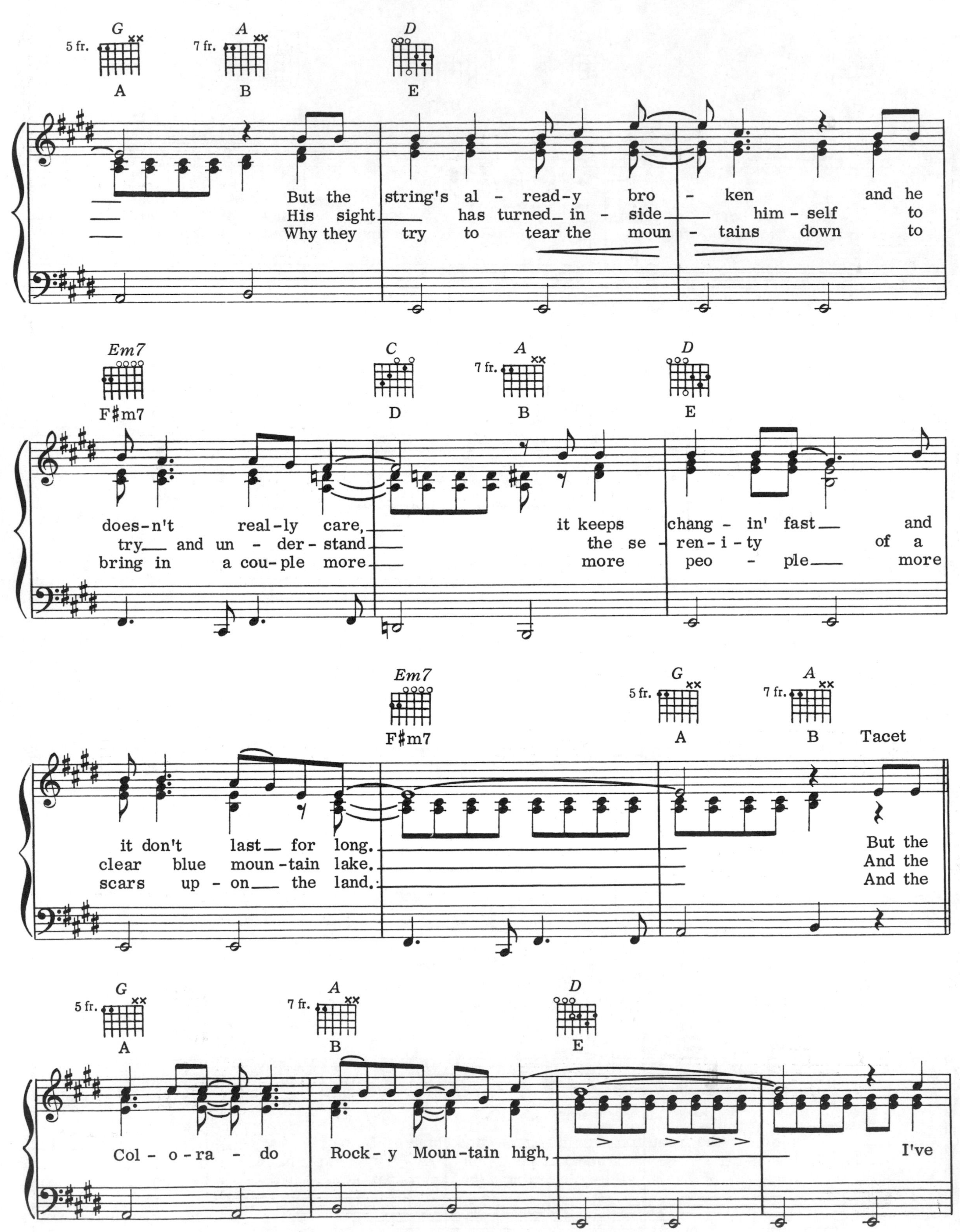
G
5 fr.
A
7 fr.
D
A
B
E
But the string's al - read - y bro - ken and he
His sight has turned in - side him - self to
Why they try to tear the moun - tains down to
Em7
C
A
7 fr.
D
F♯m7
D
B
E
does-n't real-ly care, it keeps chang - in' fast and
try and un - der - stand the se - ren - i - ty of a
bring in a cou-ple more more peo - ple more
Em7
G
5 fr.
A
7 fr.
F♯m7
A
B
Tacet
it don't last for long. But the
clear blue moun-tain lake. And the
scars up - on the land. And the
G
5 fr.
A
7 fr.
D
A
B
E
Col - o - ra - do Rock - y Moun-tain high, I've

G
5 fr.
A
7 fr.
D
A
B
E
seen it rain - in' fire in the sky.
G
5 fr.
A
7 fr.
A
B
The shad - ow from the star - light is
Talk to God and lis - ten to the cas -
I know he'd be a poor - er man if he
D
Pull off
1st finger
Em7
Dmaj7
G
5 fr.
E
F♯m7
Emaj7
A
soft - er than a lull - a - by.
- u - al re - ply.
nev - er saw an ea - gle fly.
mp
D
P.O.
E
Em7
F♯m7
Rock - y Moun - tain high,
mf

G
A
D
5 fr.
7 fr.
A
B
To Coda
E
Rock-y Moun-tain high
Em7
1.
G
A
2.
G
A
F#m7
A
B
A
B
D. S. al Coda
He climbed
Now his life
Coda
D
G
5 fr.
E
A
It's a Col-o-ra-do Rock-
f
A
D
7 fr.
B
E
-y Moun-tain high,
I've

G
5 fr.
A
7 fr.
D
A
B
E
seen it rain-in' fire in the sky.
G
5 fr.
A
7 fr.
D
Em7
D
A
B
E
F#m7
E
Friends a-round the camp - fire and ev - 'ry - bod - y's
dim. poco
G
5 fr.
A
high.
Rock-y Moun-tain high,
a poco
mp mf
D
Em7
G
5 fr.
A
7 fr.
Repeat and Fade
E
F#m7
A
B
Rock-y Moun-tain high,

Seasons In The Sun (Le Moribond)

English Lyric by Rod McKuen
Music by Jacques Brel

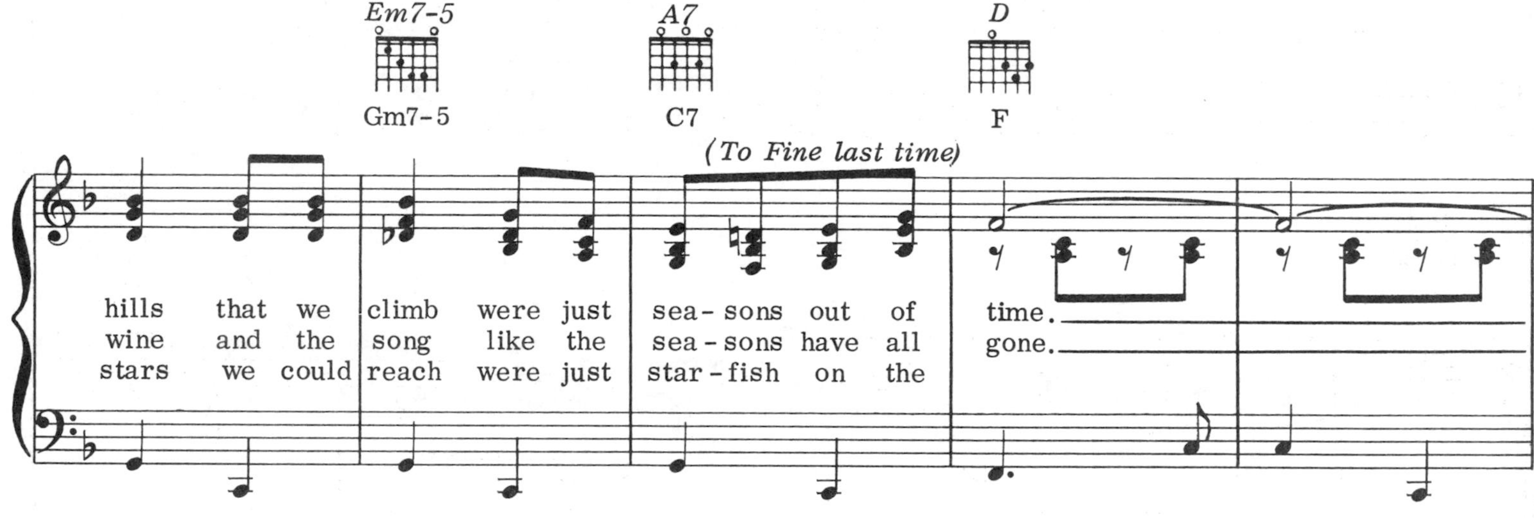

Verse
D F A7 C7
1. Good-bye to you, my trust-ed friend,
2. Good-bye, Pa-pa, please pray for me,
3. Good-bye, Mich-elle, my lit-tle one,
mp
F F G 3 fr. B♭
We've known each oth-er since we were nine or ten;
I was the black sheep of the fam-i-ly;
You gave me love and helped me find the sun;
Gm 3 fr. B♭m D F A7 C7
To-geth-er we've climbed hills and trees,
You tried to teach me right from wrong,
And ev-'ry time that I was down,
D F G 3 fr. B♭ Gm 3 fr. B♭m
Learned of love and A-B-C's, skinned our hearts and skinned our
Too much wine and too much song, won-der how I got a-
You would al-ways come a-round and get my feet back on the

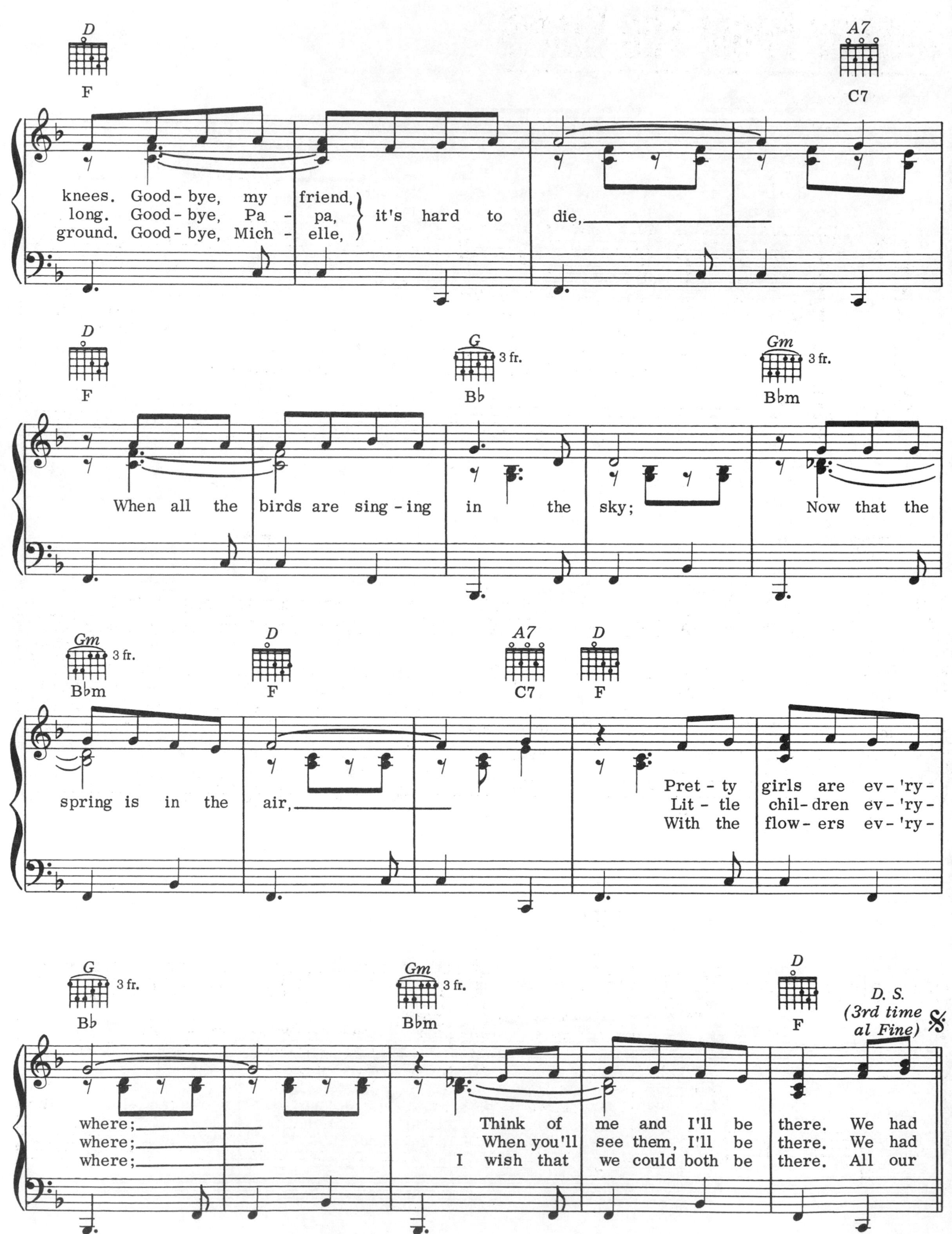
D F A7 C7
knees. Good-bye, my friend,
long. Good-bye, Pa - pa,
ground. Good-bye, Mich - elle,
it's hard to die,
D F G 3 fr. B♭ Gm 3 fr. B♭m
When all the birds are sing-ing in the sky; Now that the
Gm 3 fr. B♭m D F A7 C7 D F
spring is in the air,
Pret-ty girls are ev-'ry-
Lit-tle chil-dren ev-'ry-
With the flow-ers ev-'ry-
G 3 fr. B♭ Gm 3 fr. B♭m D F
D. S. (3rd time al Fine)
where; Think of me and I'll be there. We had
where; When you'll see them, I'll be there. We had
where; I wish that we could both be there. All our

Shelter From The Storm

Words and Music by Bob Dylan

G
D
crea-ture void of form
al-ways safe and warm
took my crown of thorns
blows a fu-tile horn
got re-paid with scorn
"Come in," she said, "I'll give you
G
D
G
D
Shel-ter from the storm."
1. And
2. I was
3.4.5.
D
G
if I pass this way a-gain
burned out from ex-haus-tion
Now there's a wall be-tween us
I've heard new-born ba-bies wail-in'
Well, I'm liv-in' in a for-eign coun-try But I'm
You can rest as-
Bur-ied in the
Some-thin' there's been
Like a morn-in'
bound to cross the
D
sured I'll al-ways do my best for her On
hail Poi-soned in the bush-es An'
lost I took too much for grant-ed
dove And old men with bro-ken teeth
line Beau-ty walks a ra-zor's edge Some-

G
D
that I give__ my word. In a world of steel - eyed
blown out on____ the trail. Hunt - ed like a
Got my sig - nals crossed. Just to think that it
Strand - ed with - out love. Do I un - der - stand your
day I'll make__ it mine. If I could on - ly turn
G
death and men__ Who are fight - ing to be warm____
croc - o - dile__ Rav - aged in the corn____
all be - gan__ On a long for - got - ten morn____
ques - tion, man__ Is it hope - less and for - lorn____
back the clock_ To when God and her were born____
"Come
D
G
D
in," she said, "I'll give___ you Shel-ter from__ the storm."__
1. 2. 3. 4.
5.
G
D
G
D
2. Not a
3. Sud - den-
4. Well, the
5. In a
rit.

Space Oddity

Words and Music by David Bowie

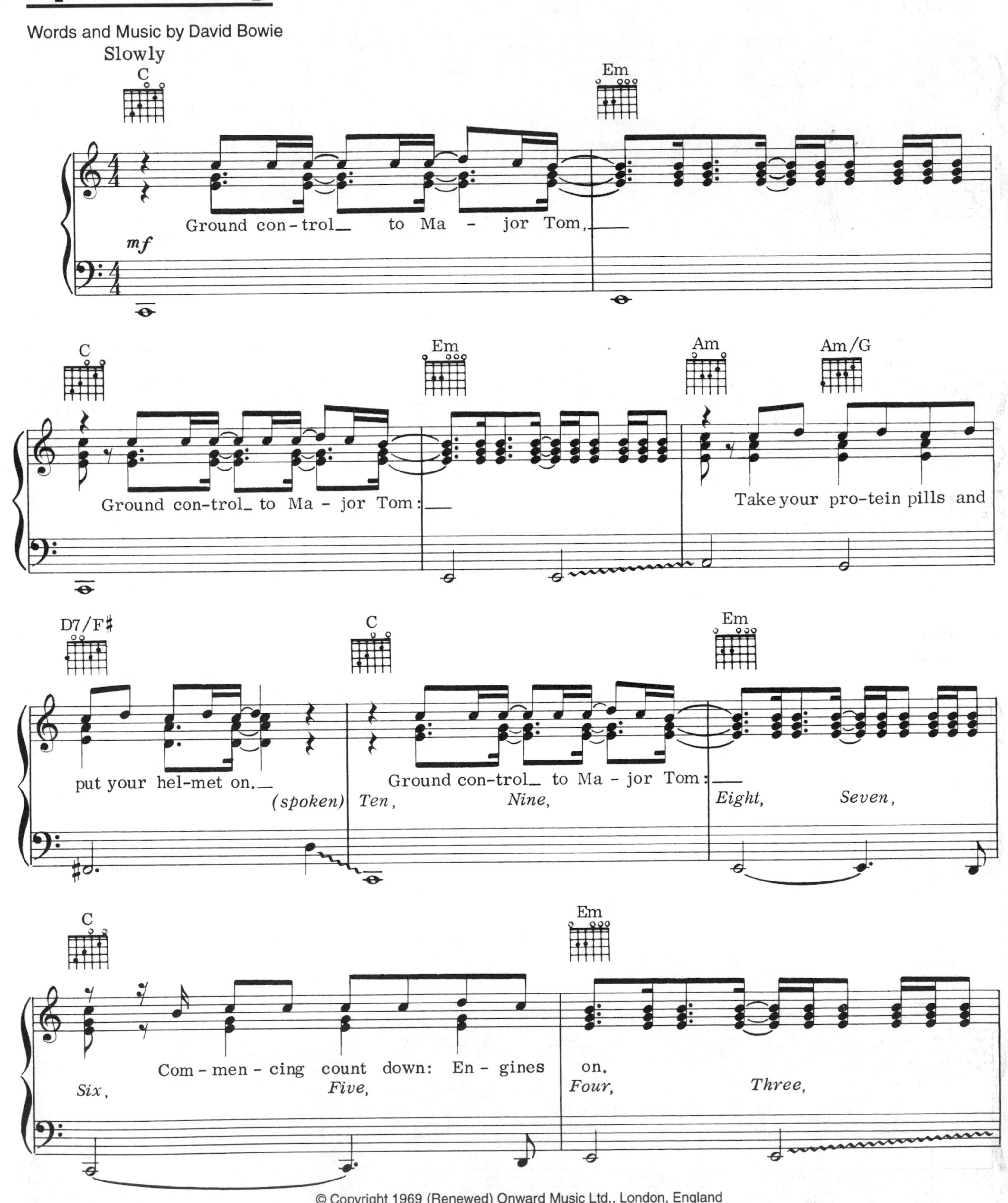

Am
Am/G
D7/F♯
C9+11
Check ig - ni - tion and may God's love be with you.
Two, One, Lift off!
Space-craft lift off music
C
E7
This is ground con-trol to Ma - jor Tom; You've real - ly made the grade!
This is Ma - jor Tom to ground con-trol; I'm step - ping through the door,
f
F
Fm
C/E
And the pa - pers want to know whose shirts you wear.
And I'm float - ing in a most pe - cul - iar way.
F
Fm
C/E
F
Now it's time to leave the cap - sule if you dare
And the stars look ver - y dif - fer - ent to - day
2nd (For)

Fmaj7
Em7
Fmaj7
here am I sit-ting in a tin can
Here am I float-ing round my tin can
Far a-bove the world
Far a-bove the moon
Em7
B♭maj7
Amadd 9
Gadd 9
Plan-et Earth is blue and there's noth-ing I can
Plan-et Earth is blue and there's noth-ing I can
F
N. C.
Last time to Coda
do.
do.
f
C
E7
Though I'm past one hun-dred thou-sand miles
I'm feel-ing ver-y still

F
Fm
C/E
F
And I think my space-ship knows which way to go
Tell my
Fm
C/E
F
wife I love her ver-y much "She knows"
G
E7-9
Am
Am/G
"Ground con-trol to Ma-jor Tom: Your cir-cuit's dead. There's some-thing wrong. Can you
D7/F♯
C/G
hear me, Ma-jor Tom? Can you hear me, Ma-jor Tom? Can you
G
D. S. al Coda
hear me, Ma-jor Tom? Can you"
Coda
Eadd 9
gliss.

From the Paramount Picture THE GODFATHER

Speak Softly, Love (Love Theme)

Words by Larry Kusik
Music by Nino Rota

Slowly

mf

Cm 3 fr. | Fm/C | Cm 3 fr.

mp

Speak soft-ly love and hold me warm a-gainst your heart, I feel your

Fm

words the ten-der trem-bling mo-ments start. We're in a world, our ver-y

mf

Cm 3 fr. | Cm/G 3 fr. | G7sus4 3 fr. | G7 3 fr. | Cm 3 fr.

own, Shar-ing a love that on-ly few have ev-er known. Wine col-ored

f

Bb7
6 fr.
Ebmaj7
6 fr.
Db/F
days warmed by the sun; Deep vel-vet nights when we are
G7
N.C.
Cm
3 fr.
Fm/C
Cm
3 fr.
one. Speak soft-ly, love, so no one hears us but the sky, The vows of
Fm
love we make will live un-til we die. My life is yours and all be-
Cm
3 fr.
Cm/G
3 fr.
Fm6/G
G7
Cm
3 fr.
cause You came in-to my world with love, so soft-ly love.
slower

Sunshine On My Shoulders

Words by John Denver
Music by John Denver, Mike Taylor and Dick Kniss

G C G C G C G C
B♭ E♭ B♭ E♭ B♭ E♭ B♭ E♭
To Coda
sun-shine almost al-ways makes me high.
G Am7 Bm C G Am7
B♭ Cm7 Dm E♭ B♭ Cm7
If I had a day that I could give you,
If I had a tale that I could tell you,
Bm C G Am7 Bm C
Dm E♭ B♭ Cm7 Dm E♭
3
I'd give to you a day just like to-
I'd tell a tale sure to make you
Am7 D7 G Am7
Cm7 F7 B♭ Cm7
day.
smile.
If I had a
If I had a

Bm
C
G
Am7
Bm
C
Dm
E♭
B♭
Cm7
Dm
E♭
song that I could sing for you, I'd
wish that I could wish for you, I'd
G
Am7
Bm
C
G
Am7
Bm
C
B♭
Cm7
Dm
E♭
B♭
Cm7
Dm
E♭
Last time, D.S. 𝄋 al 𝄌 Coda
sing a song to make you feel this way.
make a wish for sun-shine all the while.
Coda
G
C
G
C
G
Am7
Bm
C
B♭
E♭
B♭
E♭
B♭
Cm7
Dm
E♭
Sun-shine al-most all the time makes me high,
G
C
G
C
G
Am7
Bm
C
G
B♭
E♭
B♭
E♭
B♭
Cm7
Dm
E♭
B♭
sun-shine al-most al-ways...

Take Me Home, Country Roads

Words and Music by John Denver, Bill Danoff and Taffy Nivert

D
E
C
D
G
A
young - er than the moun - tains grow - in' like a breeze.
mist - y taste of moon - shine, tear - drop in my eye.
G
A
D
E
Coun - try Roads, take me home to the
Em
F♯m
C
D
G
A
place I be - long: West Vir - gin - ia,
D
E
C
D
mountain mom - ma, Take me home, Coun - try
G
A
1.
2. Em
F♯m
D
E
Roads. All my I hear her voice, in the

G C G
A D A
morn - in' hours she calls me, the ra - di - o re - minds me of my
D Em F C
E F♯m G D
home far a - way, and driv - in' down the road I get a feel - in' that I
G D D7
A E E7
D.S. 𝄋 al Coda ⊕
should have been home yes - ter - day, yes - ter - day.
Coda
G D G
A E A
Roads, take me home, Coun-try Roads,
D G
E A
take me home, Coun-try Roads.

Superstar

Words and Music by Leon Russell and Bonnie Bramlett

Chorus
Dm
Eb
3 fr.
5 fr.
Cm
ra - di - o.
sad gui - tar.
Don't you re - mem - ber you told me you love me, ba -
Bb
4 fr.
Ab
- by?
You said you'd be com - ing back this way a - gain may - be.
Ba - by, ba - by, ba - by, ba - by, oh, ba - by, I love you,
1.
2.
Ebmaj7
Gm
Dm (add 9)
I real - ly do.
mp
I real - ly do.

Sweet Baby James

Words and Music by James Taylor

Bb
F
C7
Gm7
Wait - ing for sum - mer his pas - tures to change.
ten miles be - hind me and ten thou-sand more to go.
C
Gm7
C
Bb
And as the moon
There's a song that they
Gm7/C
Fadd 9
Dm
ris - es he sits by his fire Think - ing 'bout
sing when they take to the high - way, A song that they
Bb
F
C
Bb
wom - en and glass - es of beer And clos - ing his
sing when they take to the sea, A song that they

Gm7/C
Fadd9
Dm
eyes as the do - gies re - tire, He sings out a
sing of their home in the sky, May - be you can be -
B♭
F
Am
Dm7
song which is soft but it's clear, As if may - be
lieve it if it helps you to sleep, But sing - ing works
G7
Gm7/C
C7
some - one could hear:
just fine for me.
F
B♭
Gm7/C
F
Good - night, you moon - light la - dies,
mf

Dm
Bb
F
Rock - a - bye, sweet Ba - by James.
Dm
Bb
F
F/E
Deep greens and blues are the col - ors I choose Won't you
Dm7
G7
Gm7/C
C7
let me go down in my dreams, And
Bb
C7
F
1.
2.
rock - a - bye sweet Ba - by James. Now the

Thank God I'm A Country Boy

Words and Music by John Martin Sommers

A E7 A
God I'm a coun-try boy. A sim-ple kind-a life nev-er
God I'm a coun-try boy. I'd play "Sal-ly Goodin'" all
God I'm a coun-try boy. Yeah, cit-y folk drivin' in a
God you're a coun-try boy. My dad-dy taught me young how to
D A
did me no harm, rais-in' me a fam-i-ly and
day if I could, but the Lord and my wife would-n't
black limou-sine, A lot-ta sad peo-ple think-in'
hunt and how to whittle, He taught me how to work and play a
G E7 A
work-in' on a farm. My days are all filled with an
take it ver-y good. So I fid-dle when I can and I
that's might-y keen. Well, folks, let me tell you now ex-
tune on the fiddle. He taught me how to love and how to
D A E7 A
(4th time only)
eas-y coun-try charm: Thank God I'm a coun-try boy.
work when I should: Thank God I'm a coun-try boy.
act-ly what I mean: I thank God I'm a coun-try boy.
give just a little: Thank God I'm a coun-try boy.
Well, I
(4th time)

E
A
got me a fine wife, I got me old fid - dle. When the
E
A
sun's com - in' up I got cakes on the grid - dle; And
D
(4th time only)
life ain't noth - in' but a fun - ny, fun - ny rid - dle: Thank
(4th time)
1. 2. 3.
4.
A
E7
A
A
God I'm a coun - try boy.
2. When the
3. I
4. Well, my

From the Musical Production ANNIE

Tomorrow

Lyric by Martin Charnin
Music by Charles Strouse

With a lilt
mf
F
Fmaj7
The sun - 'll come out to - mor - row,
B♭maj7
Am7
Dm
Dm/C
B♭maj7
C
bet your bot- tom dol- lar that to- mor-row there'll be sun! Jus'
F
Fmaj7
B♭maj7
Am7
think- ing a - bout to - mor - row clears a-way the cob - webs and the

Dm
Dm/C
Bbmaj7
C7sus4
sor - row till there's none. When I'm stuck with a
Fm
Fm/Eb
Db
Eb
3 fr.
Ab
4 fr.
Abmaj7
3 fr.
day that's gray and lone - ly, I just stick out my chin and grin and
C7sus4
C7
N.C.
F
Fmaj7
say: Oh! The sun 'll come out to- mor-row,
mp sub.
Bbmaj7
Am7
Dm
Dm/C
Gbmaj7
C7sus4
C7
So you
Oh! I
got to hang on till to- mor-row come what may! To -

F
Fmaj7
F7
B♭
F
C7sus4
C7
mor-row, to-mor-row, I love ya to-mor-row, you're
al-ways
on-ly
a day a-
1.
F
Fmaj7
B♭maj7/F
C7sus4/G
way!
The
2.
F
C7sus4
way! To-
F
Fmaj7
F7
B♭
F
C7sus4
mor-row, to-mor-row, I love ya to-mor-row, you're
al-ways
on-ly
a day a-
F
Fmaj7
B♭maj7/F
C7sus4/G
F
way!

Time In A Bottle

Words and Music by Jim Croce

D
D/C#
D/B
D/A
nev - er seems to be e-nough time To do the things you want to do once you
G
G/F#
Em7
A7
D
find them. I've looked a-round e -
D/C#
D/B
D/A
G
nough to know that you're the one I want to go thru time with.
G/F#
Em7
A7
To Coda
D. S. al Coda
If
Coda
A7
Dm

Torn Between Two Lovers

Words and Music by Peter Yarrow and Phillip Jarrell

Am
C
Am7
D
Cm
E♭
Cm7
F
hold you close and say these words as gent-ly as I can.
Am7
D7
G
Cm7
F7
B♭
There's been an-oth-er man that I've need-ed and I've loved,
You must-n't think you failed me just be-cause there's some-one else, You were the
Am7
D7
G
Cm7
F7
B♭
But that does-n't mean I love you less. And he
first real love I ev-er had.
Am7
D7
G
Em
Cm7
F7
B♭
Gm
knows he can't pos-sess me, and he knows he nev-er will, There's just this
And all the things I ev-er said, I swear they still are true For
I could-n't real-ly blame you if you turned and walked a-way, But with

Am C Am D
Cm E♭ Cm F
emp - ty place__ in - side of me that on - ly he can fill.
no one else__ can have the part of me I gave to you.
ev - 'ry - thing__ in - side of me, I'm ask - ing you to stay.
Chorus
Am D7 Bm E7 Am7 D7
Cm F7 Dm G7 Cm7 F7
Torn be - tween two lov - ers,__ Feel - ing__ like a fool, Lov - ing both of you__ is
G E7 Am D7 Bm E7
B♭ G7 Cm F7 Dm G7
break - ing all__ the rules. Torn be - tween two lov - ers,__ Feel - ing like a fool,
Am7 D7 G
Cm7 F7 B♭
After repeat, D. S. 𝄋
and fade on Chorus
Lov - ing you both is break - ing all__ the rules.

From the Motion Picture THE WAY WE WERE

The Way We Were

Words by Alan and Marilyn Bergman
Music by Marvin Hamlisch

Dmaj7
E7sus
E7
1
Amaj7
F♯m7
Bm7
D/E
of the way we were.
for the way we
Scat-tered
2
Amaj7
A7
Dmaj7
C♯m7 Bm7
were.
Can it be that it was all so sim-ple then,
C♯m7
F♯7sus
F♯7
Bm7
Bm7/A
or has time re-writ-ten ev-'ry line?
If we had the chance to do it
E7sus
E7
Amaj7
D/E
E7
D.S. al Coda
all a-gain, tell me would we?
Could we?

CODA
Dmaj7
C♯7sus
C♯7
F♯m7
F♯m/E
Dmaj7
we sim-ply choose to for - get.
So it's the
C♯m7
4fr
Dmaj7
C♯m7
4fr
laugh - ter we will re - mem - ber,
Dmaj7
C♯m7
4fr
F♯m7
Bm7
2fr
Bm7/E
when - ev - er we re - mem - ber the way we
Amaj7
Dmaj7
D/E
A
Dmaj7
Amaj7
were; the way we were.
rit.

From A CHORUS LINE

What I Did For Love

Music by Marvin Hamlisch
Lyric by Edward Kleban

2.
G
G/F
G/E
G/D
Am
Am/G
love.
cresc.
Gone,
f
Fmaj7
E7sus4
E7
Am
Am/G
Am/F♯
B7sus4
B7
love is nev-er
gone,
As we trav-el
Emadd9
Em
G/A
A7
Dm7-5
on,
love's what we'll re-mem-ber.
G7
N. C.
Cadd9
C
A7sus4
A7
Kiss to-day good-bye,
mp
and point me t'ward to-

Dm7
Fm
C
G/B
mor-row.
Wish me luck, the same to
Am
Am/G
D7/F♯
Am7/E
D7
F
C/E
you.
Won't for-get, can't re-gret What I did
cresc.
f
Dm7
G7sus
G7
C
C/B♭
Fm/A♭
N. C.
for
love.
What I did for
mf
C
C/B♭
Fm/A♭
N. C.
C
love
What I did for
love.
p rall.
pp

When I Paint My Masterpiece

Words and Music by Bob Dylan

E7
A
Got to hur-ry on back to my ho-tel room, Where I've
Train wheels run-nin' through the back of my mem-o-ry, When I
News - pa - per - men eat-ing can - dy
E7
A
D
got me a date with Bot-ti - cel-li's niece. She
ran on the hill - top fol-low-ing a pack of wild geese.
Had to be held down by big po- lice.
A
D
To Coda
A
D
3
prom - ised that she'd be right there with me When I
Some - day, ev-'ry-thing is gon - na be smooth like a rhap - so-dy, When I
Some - day, ev-'ry-thing is gon - na be
A/E
E
1.
A
D
2.
A
paint my mas - ter-piece. Oh, the
paint my mas - ter-piece.

Dm
A
Sail-in' 'round the world in a dirt-y gon-do-la.
C♯m
4 fr.
D
E
D
Oh, to be back in the land of Co-ca Co-la!
A/C♯
Cdim
E7
D. S. al Coda
I left
Coda
A
D
dif-f'rent
A/E
E
D
A/C♯
Bm
A
When I paint my mas-ter-piece.
R. H.
rit.

From the Paramount Picture LOVE STORY

Where Do I Begin (Love Theme)

Words by Carl Sigman
Music by Francis Lai

Slowly
Gm
F♯dim7/G
E♭maj7
p
With pedal
D7sus
D7
Gm
mp
Where do I be - gin to tell the sto - ry of how
With her first hel - lo she gave a mean - ing to this
D7
great a love can be, the sweet love sto - ry that is
emp - ty world of mine. There'd nev - er be an - oth - er
Gm
E♭maj7
old - er than the sea, the sim - ple truth a - bout the
love, an - oth - er time; she came in - to my life and

D7
1
Gm
3 fr
love she brings to me?
made the liv - ing fine.
Where do I start?
F♯dim7/G
2
Gmaj7
She fills my heart.
mf
G7
Cm
3 fr
F7
She fills my heart with ver - y spe - cial things, with an - gel
B♭maj7
E♭maj7
3 fr
Am7♭5
D7
songs, with wild i - mag - in - ings. She fills my soul with so much

Gm
Cm
love that an - y - where I go I'm nev - er
F7
B♭maj7
lone - ly. With her a - long, who could be
E♭
A7
Dmaj7
lone - ly? I reach for her hand; it's al - ways there.
D7
Gm
How long does it last? Can love be meas - ured by the
mp

D7
Gm
hours _ in a day? ___ I have no an-swers now, but this much I can say:
E♭maj7
3 fr
D7
I know I'll need her till the stars all burn a - way, ___ and she'll be
rall.
Gm
F♯dim7/G
there. ___
p a tempo
E♭maj7
D7sus
D7
Gm
rit.

Where Is The Love?

Words and Music by Ralph MacDonald and William Salter

F6
Gb6
Bbmaj7
Cbmaj7
G/A
3fr.
Ab/Bb
ev - er be?
just a lie?
Where is the love?
Where is the love?
Dmaj7
Ebmaj7
You told me that you did - n't love him, and you were gon - na say good -
If you had had a sud - den change of heart, I wish that you would tell me
Oh, how I wish I'd nev - er met you. I guess it must have been my
bye.
so.
fate
But if you real - ly did - n't mean it,
Don't leave me hang - ing on to prom - is - es.
to fall in love with some - one else - 's love.

G/A
3fr.
A♭/B♭
To Coda
1.
2.
why did you have to lie?
You've got to let me know.
All I can do is wait.
Dmaj7
E♭maj7
D7
E♭7
Do do do do,
do do do do,
G6
A♭6
C7
D♭7
F6
G♭6
do do do do do do do;
do do do do

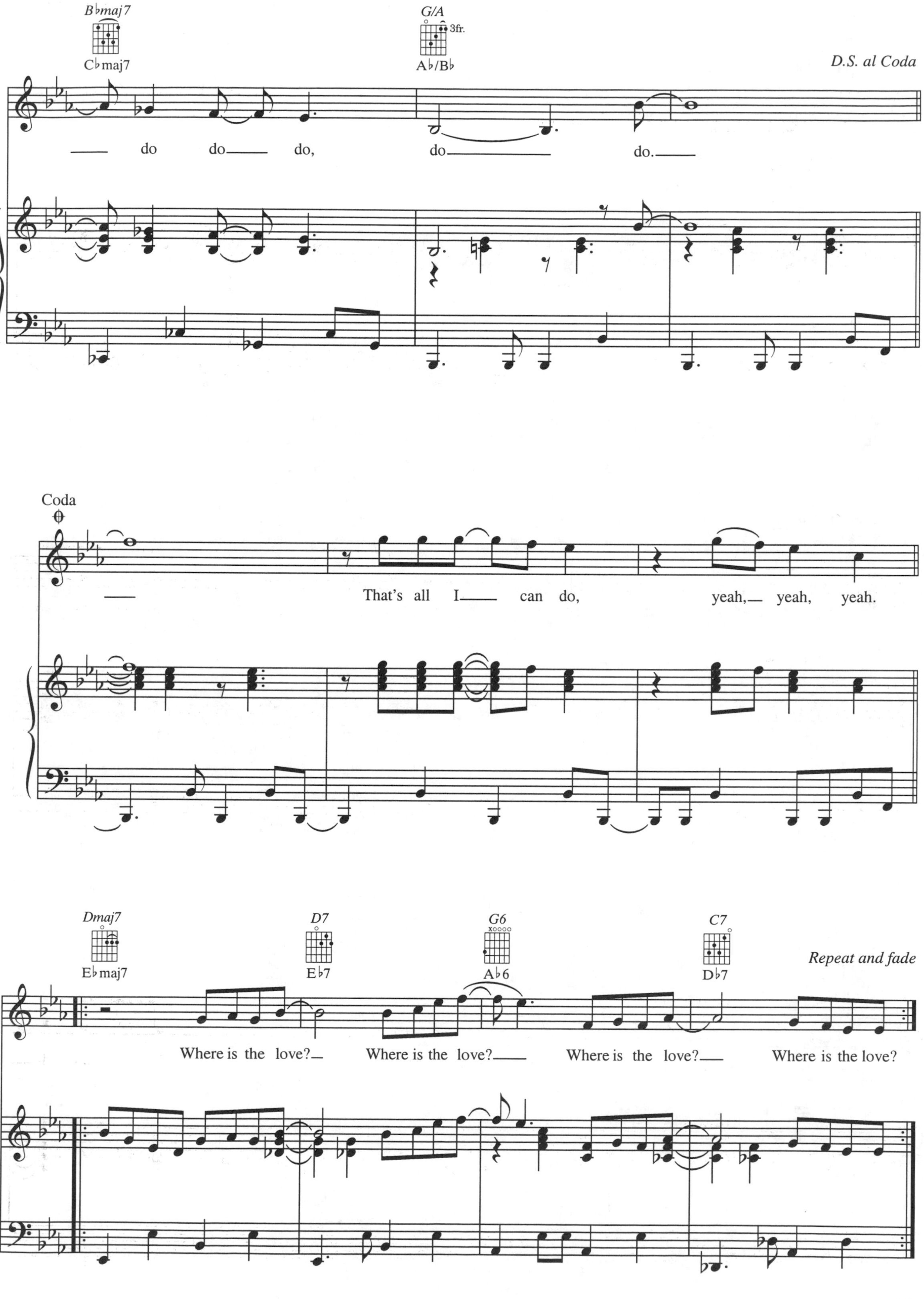

Coda

That's all I can do, yeah, yeah, yeah.

Dmaj7 D7 G6 C7

E♭maj7 E♭7 A♭6 D♭7

Repeat and fade

Where is the love? Where is the love? Where is the love? Where is the love?

You Are The Sunshine Of My Life

Words and Music by Stevie Wonder

F6
Em7
G♭/B♭
6fr
- ple of my eye.
Dm7
Dm/G
C
For - ev - er you'll stay in my heart,
Dm7
D♭m7
C
F6
F/G
I feel like this is the be -
You must have known that I was
Cmaj7
F9
F/G
Cmaj7
- gin - ning,
lone - ly,
'though I've loved you
be - cause you came

F
F/G
E7/B
Em
E+
E
for a mil - lion years.
to my res - cue.
A
D
E
Am
And if I thought our love was end - ing,
And I know that this must be hea - ven;
D7
I'd find my - self drown - ing in my own
how could so much love be in - side of
G7
1,2
(2nd time)
Repeat and Fade
Optional Ending
Cmaj7
tears. Whoa, whoa.
you? Whoa.

You Make Me Feel Like Dancing

Words and Music by Vini Poncia and Leo Sayer

E♭
3 fr.
F
I'm in a spin, you know; shak - ing on a string, you know.
You put a spell on me; I'm right where you want me to be.
cresc.
G
3 fr.
G/F♯
G/E
G/D
Am7
D11
5 fr.
You make me feel like dancing; I wan-na dance the night a-way.
You make me feel like dancing; I wan-na dance my life a-way.
f
G
3 fr.
G/F♯
G/E
G/D
Am7
D11
5 fr.
You make me feel like dancing; I'm gon-na dance the night a-way.
You make me feel like dancing; I wan-na dance my life a-way.
G
3 fr.
G/F♯
G/E
G/D
Am7
D11
5 fr.
You make me feel like danc - ing. I feel like

Gm7
3 fr.
danc - ing,
danc - ing,
dance the night a-way.
I feel like
C11
danc - ing,
danc - ing,
ah.
F
Dm7
1. 2.
Gm7
3 fr.
C11
3.
Gm7
3 fr.
C11
mf
E♭
3 fr.
F
D. S. and fade
And if you'll let me stay,
we'll dance our lives a - way.
cresc.

From SATURDAY NIGHT FEVER

You Should Be Dancing

Words and Music by Barry Gibb, Maurice Gibb and Robin Gibb

Moderately, with a beat

Cm
Cm/B
Cm/B♭
Cm/B
do - in' on your back,
aah,
what you
Cm
Cm/B
Cm/B♭
Cm/B
do - in' on your back,
aah?
You should be
Gm
3 fr.
danc - in',
yeah,
1.
2.
D. S. and fade
danc - in',
yeah.
She's
What you

From GREASE

You're The One That I Want

Words and Music by John Farrar

Moderately
Am
I got chills. They're mul - ti - ply - in'.
filled with af - fec - tion
f
F
C
And I'm los - in' con - trol.
you're too shy to con - vey,
E
Am
'Cause the pow - er you're sup - ply - in',
med - i - tate in my di - rec - tion.

it's e - lec - tri - fy - in'!
Feel your way.
C
You bet - ter shape up, 'cause I need
I bet - ter shape up, 'cause you need
Em
Am
a man and my heart is set on
a man who can keep you sat - is -
F
C
you. You bet - ter shape up;
fied. I bet - ter shape up

Em
you bet - ter un - der - stand
if I'm gon - na prove
Am
F
to my heart I must be true.
that your faith is jus - ti - fied.
Noth - in'
Are you
left, noth - in' left for me to do.
sure? Yes, I'm sure down deep in - side.
You're the
C
one that I want.
You, oo,

F
C
oo, hon - ey. The one that I want.
F
C
You, oo, oo, hon - ey. The one that I want.
F
G
x000
You, oo, oo are what I need.
1.
2.
D. S. 𝄋 and fade
Oh, yes in - deed. If you're You're the

You've Got A Friend

Words and Music by Carole King

Gm7
3fr
C7
Fm
C7
close your eyes _ and think of me and soon I ___ will be there _
keep your head _ to - geth - er and call my ___ name out loud; _
Fm/A♭
C7/G
Fm
B♭m7
Cm7
3fr
___ to bright - en up ___ e - ven your dark - est night. _
___ soon you'll hear _ me ___ knock-in' at ___ your door. _
B♭m7/E♭
6fr
E♭
3fr
B♭m7/E♭
6fr
N.C.
A♭
4fr
𝄋
You just call ___ out my __ name _
D♭
___ and you know _ wher-ev - er I am ___ I'll come run -

A♭
4fr
B♭m7/E♭
6fr
- nin' ___ to see you a - gain. ___
A♭
4fr
A♭maj7
Win-ter, spring, sum-mer or fall, ___
D♭
A♭6
3fr
A♭7
4fr
To Coda
1
D♭
Cm7
3fr
all you have to do is call ___ and I'll be ___ there. ___
B♭m7
B♭m7/E♭
6fr
A♭
4fr
D♭/A♭
4fr
You've got a friend. ___

Db Ab/C Bbm Ab Gm7 C7
N.C.
2
Db Cm7
If the sky there, yes, I will.
Bbm7 Bbm7/Eb Gb Db
Now ain't it good to know that you've got a friend when
Ab Abmaj7 Db
peo-ple can be so cold? They'll hurt you, yes, and de-sert
Gb7 Fm Bb7
you and take your soul if you let them. Oh, but

Bbm7/Eb
6fr
N.C.
D.S. al Coda
don't you let them.
You just call
CODA
Db
Cm7
3fr
Bbm7
Bbm7/Eb
6fr
there, yes, I will.
You've got a friend.
Ab
4fr
Db/Ab
4fr
You've got a
Ab
4fr
Db/Ab
4fr
Repeat and Fade
friend.
Ain't it good to know you've got a